Stéphane Marie

# THE MOST BEAUTIFUL GARDENS of Paris

Flammarion

Silence, ça pousse!

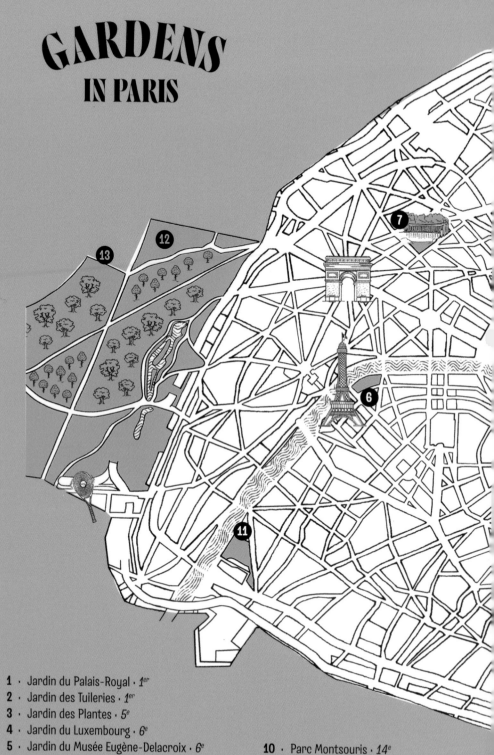

# GARDENS
## IN PARIS

# Preface

A large part of my life has been spent visiting gardens of all sorts, thanks to the years I have devoted to working on the French television show *Silence, ça pousse!* It is always such a delight to explore landscapes imagined by others and to travel through time, for each garden is steeped in history and has a unique story to tell.

Visit after visit, I am surprised—amazed, even—by the remarkable combinations of plants or of trees. And, quite simply, I love being overcome with the feeling of well-being that emanates from whichever garden I find myself in.

This book is here to guide you and help you choose the setting for your next stroll from among a selection of iconic parks in and around Paris, as well as more secret locations.

I know of no better tool than a good book to spark the imagination and encourage the curious to take a closer look. The pages of this guide are a foretaste of what awaits, and the various perspectives are sure to convince you to visit a garden or two when in Paris. The most beautiful gardens of Paris are now yours for the taking.

Stéphane Marie

# Contents

# 1

# JARDIN
## du Palais Royal
### Paris 1ᵉʳ

*This beautiful rectangular garden, bounded by Rue de Beaujolais,*
*Rue de Montpensier, and Rue de Valois, is quite peaceful.*
*It is the perfect place to stop for a rest between museum visits or after exploring*
*the neighborhood's shopping arcades. But make no mistake: for centuries the garden*
*at the Palais-Royal was one of the liveliest places in the capital.*
*Abounding with leisure and entertainments into the 19th century,*
*it has provided the backdrop for some of the most decisive events in French history.*

The present-day appearance of the garden at the Palais-Royal is the result of nearly four centuries of history. Since its creation in 1692, several garden designers have contributed their vision to the space. In the late 17th century, the renowned André Le Nôtre added his personal touch. Later, Victor Louis, the architect who designed the Comédie-Française theater, transformed the garden's structure by surrounding it with three covered passages. In the early 19th century, his successor, Pierre Fontaine, designed the large central fountain (I kid you not!). The garden has continued to evolve into the present: in 1992, the American landscape designer Mark Rudkin entirely restyled the space and jazzed up the garden's strict symmetry with paved enclosures surrounded by greenery where visitors can retreat among the flowerbeds. Today, the National Monuments Center maintains this lush space nestled in the heart of the 1st arrondissement. The institution ensures that sustainable gardening practices are used by favoring the planting of perennial vegetation. When spring arrives, the garden blooms with pink magnolias. Other flowering plants include rose bushes, dahlias, and Japanese thimbleweed, as well as ivy and honeysuckle. Arching linden trees and elm and chestnut trees delicately cast shade on the paths. •

**SO SMALL BUT SO FULL OF CHARM, THANKS TO MARK RUDKIN'S TALENT.**

# The Mark of History

····································

*Richelieu was the first to occupy the grounds. In 1634, he had the Palais-Cardinal, the future Palais-Royal, built for himself so he could live near King Louis XIII.*

····································

For centuries, the site was connected to the highest spheres of power. Louis XIV spent a portion of his childhood here: in the garden he learned to ride a horse, played in miniature forts, and even nearly drowned in the fountain! But on January 5, 1649, when he was 12 years old, a crowd invaded the palace: it was La Fronde, a revolt organized by the nobility. He was forced to flee with his mother and younger brother, and this traumatizing event explains his future preference for Versailles.

⌛ The most famous owner of the Palais-Royal was Louis Philippe II, Duke of Orléans. Following the French Revolution in 1789, he changed his last name to Égalité as a display of support for the Enlightenment thinkers. A bon vivant, he prohibited the police from entering the garden and kept it open late into the night, encouraging all manner of leisure and entertainment. From then on, an ever-expanding crowd pressed outside the restaurants, cafés, bookstores, and gaming houses in the galleries. Unusual entertainments included shadow puppetry and Philippe Curtius's museum of wax figures, a precursor to the Musée Grévin, where replicas of members of the royal family were seated around a table. The garden at the Palais-Royal—an enclave outside the reach of the law—also attracted many prostitutes.

⌛ The cafés in the galleries became the setting for impassioned political debate between philosophers and intellectuals. On July 12, 1789, after Jacques Necker, the highly popular finance minister, was dismissed, Camille Desmoulins got up on a table and rallied the crowd to take up arms against the monarchy. The rest is history. Several years later, Philippe Égalité voted in favor of executing his cousin, Louis XVI, and then—in an ironic twist—was guillotined himself.

⌛ The Palais-Royal was handed over to the French state in 1793. In the following decades, it changed hands with each succeeding political regime. The garden, which continued to be popular, was ransacked during the Revolution of 1848, then was set fire to during the Paris Commune. It gradually lost its spirited ambience and acquired a more formal atmosphere when the Council of State took up residence in the Palais-Royal in 1875, followed by the Constitutional Council in 1958.

The fan-shaped fountain in the central pool.

# Jardin Remarquable

jardin
remarquable

In 2005, the garden was awarded this distinction, meaning "Remarkable Garden": a label created by the Ministry of Culture for the most remarkable gardens and parks in France.

## THE SMALL CANNON AT THE PALAIS-ROYAL

☞ This small replica of a sundial cannon was added to the garden in 1786. It was fired every day at noon, between May and October, by concentrating the sun's rays through a small magnifying glass, which ignited the fuse. Passersby set their watches by the daily cannon shot.

# The Kraków Tree

This chestnut tree was one of the largest trees in the garden at the Palais-Royal. It wasn't actually brought from Poland though—its name comes from the fact that in the 18th century people gathered under its foliage to gossip—*raconter des craques*, in French. Paul Lacroix (1806–1884), *XVIII<sup>e</sup> siècle: Lettres, sciences et arts, France 1700–1789* (18th century: Letters, science, and art, France 1700–1789), Paris: Firmin-Didot & Cie, 1878.

Daniel Buren, *Les Deux Plateaux* (1986).

## COLONNES DE BUREN

These mysterious columns of black-and-white striped marble caused a scandal when they were installed. But what was Daniel Buren trying to express with them? In 1965, he chose to make stripes his only means of artistic expression, and he scattered them in public spaces throughout his career. They invite viewers to reflect upon their relationship to their surroundings and their expectations of art.

# An Ode to the Arts

Located near the Musée du Louvre and the Ministry of Culture, the Palais-Royal and its grounds maintain a close relationship with various forms of art. This is nothing new: in the 17th century, Cardinal Richelieu hung his remarkable painting collections in the building. Today, visitors can admire two marble statues emerging from the flowerbeds: Paul Lemoyne's *Shepherd with a Goat* (1830) and Adolphe Thabard's *Snake Charmer* (1875). The art galleries tucked under the arcades attract many painting enthusiasts.

> "IN THIS GARDEN, EVERYTHING MINGLES, EXCEPT FOR SHADE AND FLOWERS. WHILE VISITORS MAY LOSE THEIR MORAL COMPASS, AT LEAST THEY CAN SET THEIR WATCH."
> Abbot Delisle

➻ Since 1985, the main courtyard and the Galerie d'Orléans have been home to two other iconic artworks: Pol Bury's *Sphérades*—a fountain featuring large, slowly rotating silver spheres—and Daniel Buren's famous columns.

# A LITERARY ATMOSPHERE

Ever since it was created, the Palais-Royal garden has been popular with literary types. Denis Diderot went there every day, without fail, at the stroke of 5 p.m., and always sat on the same bench. In the 20th century, the area continued to attract artists and intellectuals. Colette and Jean Cocteau wrote some of their best works while living at 9 Rue de Beaujolais and 36 Rue de Montpensier respectively. Colette described herself as being "as attached to [her] Palais-Royal as a periwinkle is to its shell."

In tribute to these two authors, the Quebecois artist Michel Goulet created 18 *Eternity Laces*: these park benches have backrests engraved with quotations from their books that will impart poetic depth to any stroll.

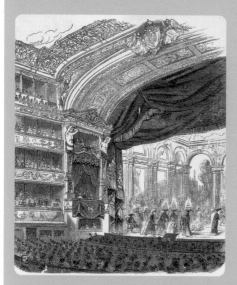

The neighborhood is also a backdrop for the dramatic arts. The first theater was built in 1627 in the Palais-Royal on Richelieu's initiative. It was there that Molière's troupe performed and where the playwright held the first performance of *The Imaginary Invalid* before he died. The Comédie-Française was built after the theater burned down in the late 18th century. Like the former theater at the Palais-Royal, it is just steps from the garden.

**"RAIN OR SHINE, IT IS MY REGULAR HABIT EVERY DAY ABOUT FIVE TO GO AND TAKE A WALK AROUND THE PALAIS-ROYAL."**
Denis Diderot

## • PRACTICAL INFORMATION •

### OPENING HOURS
October to March:
Open daily 8:30 a.m.–8:30 p.m.
April to September:
Open daily 8:30 a.m.–10:30 p.m.
Closed January 1, May 1, and December 25

### TICKETS
Free entry

### GETTING THERE
Palais Royal – Musée du Louvre (M. 1, 7)

**domaine-palais-royal.fr** (in French)

# 2

# JARDIN
# des Tuileries

## Paris 1ᵉʳ

*Ideally located between the Musée du Louvre, Musée d'Orsay,*
*Musée des Arts Décoratifs, and Place de la Concorde, the Tuileries garden*
*has played a central role in French history since it was first created.*
*In the 17th century, it was the first Parisian park open to the public.*
*Today, it welcomes visitors from around the world.*

The Tuileries garden is situated within the concentration of cultural spaces at the heart of the city. Besides the many surrounding museums—including the Louvre, the world's largest museum—the garden's neighbors include monuments like the Luxor Obelisk on Place de la Concorde, the Hôtel de la Marine, the Arc de Triomphe du Carrousel, and the Louvre Pyramid. The Eiffel Tower is visible from almost any vantage point.

❀ The epitome of the French garden, the Tuileries spans a surface area of about 62 acres (25 ha). It is crossed by a large path lined with 16 perfectly symmetrical groves, each with its own characteristics. Each end of the path leads to a pool: to the east, the round pool surrounded by an expanse of lawn that blooms with flowers in spring and summer; and to the west, the octagonal pool that leads to Place de la Concorde via horseshoe-shaped ramps. The garden is overlooked on three sides by terraces from which

visitors can admire the landscape.

🌼 In this model of harmonious balance, plants are the focus of attention. Most of the trees are pruned in architectural cuboid shapes. Some of them were planted as far back as the 19th century, during the Second Empire. The garden paths are lined with chestnut trees as well as Judas trees, orange trees in wooden planters, and elm trees—the survivors of a Dutch elm disease epidemic that wreaked havoc on the city's trees in the 1980s. One of the groves is home to a tree that differs from all the others, whose topsy-turvy roots trace the

## THIS IS LE NÔTRE'S MOST MASTERFUL USE OF PERSPECTIVE—AN OPEN-AIR MUSEUM WHERE SCULPTURES RECOUNT TALES FROM MYTHOLOGY AROUND WATER FEATURES.

forms of letters. In fact, it is *The Vowel Tree* (1919), a bronze casting by Giuseppe Penone. The flowerbeds are composed according to the seasons and the exhibitions on display at the Musée du Louvre: cosmos, dahlias, daffodils, tulips, etc.

🌼 Near the octagonal pool, two plots surrounded by pruned box trees stand out for their splendor and fragrance: these are the recently restored rose gardens, home to dozens of varieties of roses, blue sage, lady's glove, and lavender. As with the rest of the garden, they are cultivated with sustainable gardening practices. •

André Le Nôtre, Louis XIV's famous gardener, shaped the garden's current appearance. The result was so successful that the finance minister Colbert wanted to keep it closed to the public, for fear that people would damage it. But Charles Perrault, best known for his fairy tales, convinced him to make it the city's first public garden.

In the 16th century, following the death of King Henry II, the regent Catherine de Medici expressed her wish to build a royal residence near the Louvre. Construction of the Palais des Tuileries—so named in reference to the tile (*tuile*) factories that were located on the site in the Middle Ages—began in 1564. The first garden was Italian in style and featured a grotto with walls covered in work by Bernard Palissy. This renowned French ceramist invented a highly particular decorative style swarming with animal motifs (frogs, snakes, fish) cast from actual specimens. If it had survived to the present day, this grotto might not be to everyone's liking.

At the end of the 16th century, Henry IV began a wild endeavor: he wanted to connect the Louvre to the Palais de Tuileries by two seemingly endless facades. This *Grand Dessein*, as he referred to the project, would not be completed until the reign of Napoleon III and explains why the wings of the Musée du Louvre are so long.

The Palais des Tuileries remained a royal residence. During the French Revolution, Louis XVI, Marie Antoinette, and their children were placed under house arrest there, where they spent many anguished months. During the Reign of Terror, the garden played host to strange ceremonies in praise of the Supreme Being, a universal deity worshipped by Enlightenment thinkers. On June 8, 1794, allegories of Ambition, Egoism, Discord, and False Simplicity were burned above one of the pools.

The Palais des Tuileries was permanently destroyed by a fire in 1871, during the reign of the Paris Commune.

PARIS ET SES RUINES.

**PALAIS DES TUILERIES**

# THE RED PHANTOM OF THE TUILERIES

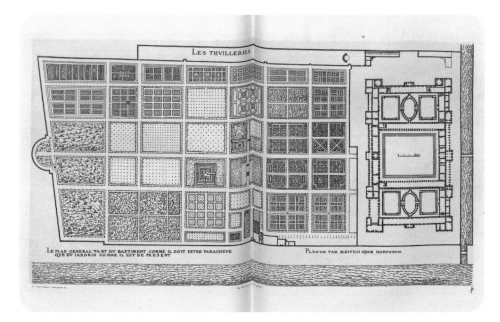

↳ The story goes that when the Palais des Tuileries was built, a certain Jean the Flayer, a butcher by trade, was executed by Catherine de Medici's enforcer for refusing to leave the worksite. He is said to have reappeared before the man as a ghost covered in blood. The red phantom, like Belphegor, his neighbor in the Louvre, was spotted several times in the following centuries. Napoleon, for example, is said to have seen him before the defeat at Waterloo.

Small sailboats at the Tuileries pool.

# An Open-Air Museum

The Tuileries garden contains 174 sculptures in a wide range of styles. Fourteen percent are casts or copies of originals that have been placed in museums, safe from inclement weather conditions and bird attacks. Every October, during the international contemporary art fair, works of contemporary art spring up along the pathways.

Aristide Maillol, *The Three Nymphs* (c. 1930). These three young women are believed to represent wildflowers: daisies, buttercups, and marjoram. The sculpture is located between the Louvre and the Tuileries.

Jean-Baptiste Hugues, *Man and His Misery* (c. 1905).

Gabriel Pech, *Monument to the Storyteller Perrault* (c. 1905).
Charles Perrault is surrounded by one of his characters, Puss in Boots (who wears a necklace of mice), and a group of little girls thanking him for helping to make the Tuileries garden accessible to the public.

Antoine Coysevox, *Fame Riding Pegasus* (c. 1700, copy dated 1986).
The original is held at the Louvre.

Auguste Rodin, *The Kiss* (c. 1880–1890).
This statue can be seen near the Musée de l'Orangerie.

# Two Indoor Museums

..................

Located to the left of the octagonal pool, the building that houses the Musée de l'Orangerie was built in 1852 to hold orange trees during the winter. In the 1920s, on the initiative of Georges Clemenceau, the building's interior was entirely reworked to accommodate Claude Monet's incredible set of *Water Lilies*. Today, visitors can still admire these monumental paintings in rooms with curved walls specifically designed to showcase the artworks. The museum also holds a number of masterpieces

from the Paul Guillaume collection, including work by Auguste Renoir, Paul Cézanne, André Derain, Pablo Picasso, Henri (Le Douanier) Rousseau, Marie Laurencin, and Chaïm Soutine. It regularly hosts exhibitions of works by leading figures of modern art.

➻ The Jeu de Paume, located across the pool, was built in 1862. It was originally designed for playing *jeu de paume*, an early version of tennis. In the 20th century, the sport fell out of fashion and the building became an exhibition gallery. Today, it is a museum dedicated to diverse images that organizes fascinating exhibitions on photography, cinema, and contemporary art.

## THE GARDEN'S PRESTIGE

The Tuileries garden has been classified as a historical monument since 1914. Along with five other gardens in Paris, it has also received Jardin Remarquable status from the Ministry of Culture.

# • PRACTICAL INFORMATION •

### OPENING HOURS
Open daily, 24h

### TICKETS
Free entry to the garden
Musée de l'Orangerie: €12.50 | adults accompanied by children €10 |
free for visitors under 18 and EU citizens under 26
Musée du Jeu de Paume: €12 | reduced price €9 | youth price €7.50

### GETTING THERE
Tuileries (M. 1), Palais Royal—Musée de Louvre (M. 1, 7), Concorde (M. 1, 8, 12)

### AMENITIES AND ACTIVITIES
| | |
|---|---|
| Toy boats | Guided tours |
| Playgrounds | Restaurants |
| Carousels | Cafés |

louvre.fr/en/explore/the-gardens

Aristide Maillol, *Méditerranée* (1905).

# JARDIN
## des Plantes
### Paris 5ᵉ

*The Jardin des Plantes comprises 11 spaces, including an ecological garden, an alpine garden, a rose garden, a maze, and a botanical school. Although diverse in nature, the garden's amenities are dedicated to a single goal: understanding and protecting the natural world. Located in the heart of the city, the Jardin des Plantes is the headquarters of the Muséum National d'Histoire Naturelle. The garden is home to several buildings dedicated to scientific exhibitions, as well as a zoo and large greenhouses shared by hundreds of animal and plant species.*

The Jardin des Plantes has changed throughout its long history, but its scientific goal has been clear since the day it was created. Today, it remains a unique place where families, nature lovers, and researchers mingle.

⌛ In 1635, King Louis XIII founded a royal garden of medicinal plants in Paris, which later became the Jardin des Plantes. This botanical garden was primarily for growing varieties of plants with healing properties, but visitors could also attend anatomy, botany, and chemistry classes free of charge.

⌛ During the Renaissance, European encounters with distant regions of the world sparked a new thirst for knowledge among natural science enthusiasts. In the curiosity cabinets, they gathered together plants, animals, and minerals from far-flung places that

**SCIENCE, RIGOR—AND WONDERFUL SURPRISES.**

were selected for their beauty or their otherness. The institute at the royal garden inherited this appetite for collecting and classifying. Rare species from distant regions, such as coffee bushes from Java and chrysanthemums from China, were studied there and adapted to the French climate. •

In 1739, the naturalist Georges-Louis Leclerc, Count de Buffon, was appointed superintendent of the Jardin Royal. Driven by the Enlightenment spirit, he spent his life working to enlarge the garden and make it a true center for scientific research. Little by little, the Jardin des Plantes acquired new facilities until it became the garden we know today: the two large greenhouses opened in 1834 and 1836, the gallery of minerology and geology in 1841, and the gallery of zoology, now the gallery of evolution, in 1889.

A statue of Buffon. Facing the gallery of evolution, Count de Buffon, seated in an armchair, watches over his oeuvre. This bronze monument was created in his memory by Jean-Marius Carlus and inaugurated in 1909.

# The Garden's Attractions

The Jardin des Plantes affords visitors many viewpoints: perfectly symmetrical paths give way to a mountainous landscape and a romantic rose bed to a Dutch-style iris garden. The constantly refreshed flowerbeds provide endless inspiration for amateur gardeners. And the garden is home to an underground zoological library that includes hundreds of thousands of preserved animal specimens.

♥ The Jardin des Plantes is said to have inspired Charles Trenet's song "Le Jardin extraordinaire."

# SPECIALIZED GARDENS

The rose garden familiarizes visitors with the diverse forms, colors, and fragrances of the queen of flowers. Up to 390 varieties of rose wind around arches and bloom at the feet of two marble statues: Charles Dupaty's *Venus Genetrix* (1810) and Félix Sanzel's *Captive Love* (1861).

At the center of the Jardin des Plantes, the botanical school, created in the 18th century, presents hundreds of plant species, including flowers, bushes, ferns, and mosses, through selections representative of each plant family. It is also home to centuries-old trees, including a Corsican pine planted in 1774—the year Louis XVI acceded to power—whose crown was destroyed by lightning.

Visitors were not allowed into the ecological garden for a long time: access was reserved for gardeners and researchers with permission to study there. In 2004, it was opened for guided tours. Various natural environments found in the Île-de-France region, including prairies, forests, and ponds, have been recreated in this enclave.

The alpine garden, created in the 1930s, includes species from mountainous regions around the world, not only the Alps: Corsica, the Caucasus, and the Himalayas are also represented.

# AN ONLINE ENCYCLOPEDIA

☞ Numerous plant species are listed on the Jardin des Plante's website, on the page "*Plantes du Jardin*" (only available in French). Each plant boasts a page brimming with information on its origins, history, and uses. Its exact location in the garden is also included, as well as recommendations about its upkeep for gardeners.

# THE GALLERY OF EVOLUTION

This exhibition space presents 7,000 surprisingly realistic animal specimens on the march. The Muséum National d'Histoire Naturelle has other spaces scattered throughout the Jardin des Plantes, including the gallery of paleontology and comparative anatomy and the gallery of geology and minerology.

# THE ZOO

Red pandas, porcupines, orangutans, snow leopards, century-old tortoises, pythons, pink flamingos, foxes, giant kangaroos, spiders: today, the zoo is home to 500 animals representing 146 different species from around the world. Most of them live in *fabriques*, small shelters built in the early 19th century; others are housed in the vivarium, the aviary, the monkey house, or the big cat enclosure.

The zoo was created in 1793, shortly after the French Revolution, which makes it one of the oldest establishments of its kind in the world. Bernardin de Saint-Pierre, the steward of the Jardin des Plantes, initiated the zoo's creation after observing that the animals in the former royal menagerie at Versailles were dying one after the other. The survivors were among the new menagerie's first residents.

In 1827, the Egyptian statesman Muhammad Ali presented a giraffe to King Charles X of France. Zarafa, as the animal was called, became a popular attraction at the Jardin des Plantes. From 1870 to 1871, during the Franco-Prussian War, Paris was besieged, and most of the animals were eaten by the city's starving inhabitants. Throughout its history, the zoo was the setting for questionable practices—into the early 20th century, visitors could ride the elephant and the dromedary—but today it is a site for study and conservation. Most of the animals are small or medium in size, and many of them are endangered. The largest species (elephants, giraffes, lions, bears), which were too cramped in the menagerie, have been gradually relocated to the Paris Zoological Park in Vincennes.

The first chrysanthemum cuttings were brought back from China in 1789 by Pierre Blancard, a French navy captain from Marseille.

➤ At the foot of the maze, the lion fountain, designed by Henri-Alfred Jacquemart, is the largest pool in the Jardin des Plantes. It was once used for watering plants in the summer.

➤ The large aviary, designed by Alphonse Milne-Edwards and built in 1888 for the 1889 World's Fair, is still in use.

# The Greenhouses

*A row of five large greenhouses—veritable monuments in metal and glass—stands on the north side of the Jardin des Plantes. Each one contains a different microcosm: the museum's gardeners and botanists have managed to recreate the conditions typical of highly diverse ecosystems, four of which are open to the public.*

➻ The tropical greenhouse stands out for its remarkable art deco architecture. Inside, the warm, humid atmosphere is similar to a tropical jungle in the Amazon or the West Indies. Visitors wander through a vibrant spectacle of lush plants that includes banana trees, vines, and orchids of all shapes and colors.

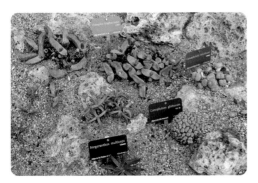

→ The second greenhouse, home to plants native to desert and arid environments, transports visitors to dry, inhospitable landscapes. Strangely shaped cacti, impressive agaves, and many other fascinating specimens await. These plants have developed unique characteristics to survive the extreme conditions typical of their habitats.

→ The New Caledonia greenhouse is home to extraordinary flora from this archipelago in the Pacific Ocean. A large portion of the species are endemic: many appeared several million years ago and today are found only in very limited areas. Majestic palm trees, giant tree-like ferns, and other botanical treasures transport visitors to the idyllic environment of New Caledonia, which is now threatened by mining and forest fires.

→ Finally, the greenhouse dedicated to the history of plants takes visitors on a journey through time, beginning 430 million years ago, when the first flora appeared, and continuing to the present day. The greenhouse enables visitors to compare current species with recreations and fossil specimens, and holds a wealth of information for understanding the way in which plants evolved along with their habitats, as well as how important they are to life on Earth.

## CHERRY BLOSSOM

As April approaches, the Japanese cherry trees bloom with pink
and white flowers, to the delight of visitors strolling through the garden.

## Buffon's Gloriette

At the top of the maze in the Jardin des
Plantes stands Buffon's gloriette, one of the
world's oldest constructions made entirely
of metal. Built in the late 18th century and
recently restored, this pavilion sometimes
shelters bats and features the inscription
*Horas non numero nisi serenas* (I only
count the joyful hours).

## • PRACTICAL INFORMATION •

### OPENING HOURS
<u>March and October:</u> Open daily 8 a.m.–6:30 p.m.
<u>April to September:</u> Open daily 7:30 a.m.–8 p.m.
<u>November to February:</u> Open daily 8 a.m.–5:30 p.m.

### TICKETS
Free entry to the Jardin des Plantes
<u>Greenhouses:</u> €9 | reduced price €7
<u>Zoo:</u> €13 | reduced price €10

### GETTING THERE
Jussieu (M. 7, 10), Saint-Marcel (M. 5), Gare d'Austerlitz
(M. 5, 10; RER C)

jardindesplantesdeparis.fr/en

# 4

# JARDIN
## du Luxembourg
### Paris 6e

*Paris is full of surprises. Did you know that the city is home to the most beautiful garden in Europe? Internet users from around the world awarded this title to the Luxembourg gardens. After strolling around the large pool, wandering along the paths, and admiring the flowerbeds, you will understand why.*

The Luxembourg gardens are located in the heart of the capital, next to the Latin quarter and its prestigious academic institutions. Within, a perfectly symmetrical French garden alternates with English gardens where nature is given more freedom. In the center of the garden, in front of the Senate building and surrounded by four large lawns, is an octagonal pool where little sailboats sometimes drift.

The iconic green chairs scattered along the paths are perfect for taking a rest or enjoying the sun. Between June and October, the dozens of flowerbeds are carefully tended to by the gardeners, who choose plant varieties based on when they bloom. During this time of the year, the pathways are always bright with an infinite variety of colorful blossoms, including forget-me-nots, primroses, dahlias, and begonias.

Nearly 3,000 trees spread their branches over the garden. Remarkable species include the handkerchief tree—named for its drooping bracts that resemble fragments of white cloth—gingko biloba, northern white cedar, and the rare white-blossomed Judas tree.

The Luxembourg gardens are also a model of sustainable management. The gardeners limit their use of chemical treatments, remove unwanted plants by hand, and practice integrated pest management, especially in the greenhouses, by using natural predators to remove aphids and other pests. •

*A STROLL THROUGH THE LUXEMBOURG GARDENS, THE MOST PARISIAN OF ALL, IS A PAUSE FROM THE WORLD.*

## THE NAME "JARDIN DU LUXEMBOURG"

❤ The garden owes its name to the former owner, the Duke de Piney-Luxembourg. Parisians sometimes refer to it as the "Luco." Contrary to popular belief, this moniker is not an abbreviation of "Luxembourg," but rather of "Lucotitius," the name of the neighborhood during antiquity—a surprisingly long-lived nickname.

# A BIT OF HISTORY

👉 In the Middle Ages, King Robert II the Pious established his residence near the site of the present-day garden, where he built the Vauvert château. After his death, the building was abandoned and fell into ruin, becoming a hot spot for beggars and miscreants.

Following a succession of prestigious owners, including Louis XIV; the regent Philippe I, Duke of Orléans; and the Count of Provence (the future Louis XVIII), the Luxembourg Palace took on a series of new roles from the French Revolution onward. It briefly served as a prison, then housed various assemblies as political upheavals succeeded one another. Under the Third Republic, the garden—now open to the public—became a favorite spot for well-off families from nearby neighborhoods to stroll. Since 1958, the palace has been the seat of the Senate of the Fifth Republic, which now manages the property.

Several centuries later, in 1610, King Henri IV was assassinated by Ravaillac on the nearby Rue de la Ferronnerie. His widow, Marie de Medici, became regent, as young Louis XIII was only eight years old. But this queen of Italian heritage was unpopular at court. She soon decided to withdraw to an estate that she purchased from the Duke de Piney-Luxembourg, and where she had a palace specially built to remind her of her native Florence.

## The Medici Fountain

☞ Around 1630, Marie de Medici had a small grotto built on the Luxembourg property. She wished to recreate the atmosphere of the Boboli Gardens in Florence, where her family had built spectacular artificial grottos decorated with 16th-century mineral sculptures.

☞ In 1862, Baron Haussmann's urban renovations led to the transformation of a large part of the Luxembourg gardens, and Marie de Medici's grotto was moved. Today, all that remains of the original monument is the facade, to which was added a 164-foot (50-m) romantic pool.

☞ The sculpture on the fountain's central alcove captures the moment preceding a terrible murder: the jealous cyclops Polyphemus is about to throw a boulder on Acis, the lover of the nymph Galatea. Auguste Ottin created this group of figures in bronze, marble, and stone in 1866.

## The Orangery

Built in 1839 and running the length of the Musée du Luxembourg, the orangery is home to more than 60 varieties of citrus trees. Some of the Seville orange trees, which produce bitter fruit, are several centuries old.

The building also holds date palms, oleanders, and pomegranates. The plants are taken outside during the summer and sheltered from the cold in winter.

Zacharie Astruc, *The Mask Seller* (1883). This young boy holds up masks of various famous figures, such as Alexandre Dumas, Victor Hugo, and Eugène Delacroix.

*The Queens of France* (1843–1877). Several statues of the queens of France and famous women, chosen by King Louis-Philippe, stand around the central pool.

The oldest carousel in Paris (1879).

Fabrice Hyber, *The Cry, The Written* (2007). This work depicts a broken chain to commemorate the abolition of slavery.

# Art in Every Corner

Besides the Musée du Luxembourg, which hosts fascinating exhibitions of painting and photography, more than 102 sculptures representing an array of historical periods populate the garden paths.

Auguste Bartholdi, *The Statue of Liberty Illuminating the World* (cast in 2011). This familiar work is a replica of a small model held at the Musée d'Orsay.

Auguste Cain, *Nubian Lion and Its Prey* (c. 1890).
A lion proudly tramples the ostrich it has just killed.

# A LITERARY PARK

👉 The Luxembourg gardens hold a prominent place in literature. They have been frequented by the greatest writers—Ernest Hemingway, for example, would regularly stroll through the park— and provided the setting for scenes in their works.

In a marvelous short story, Guy de Maupassant recounts how two elderly people meet each morning to dance the minuet in the Luxembourg nursery, before mysteriously disappearing after it is destroyed.

➻ Many of the statues that adorn the garden pay homage to writers, including the Countess of Ségur, George Sand, Paul Verlaine, Stefan Zweig, and Paul Éluard.

# Extraordinary Collections

....................................

*The Luxembourg gardens are home to several greenhouses.*

....................................

♥ One greenhouse holds the largest collection of orchids in France, which features more than 10,000 specimens in extremely varied shapes and colors. Most are tropical orchids: in their natural habitat, they usually attach themselves to tree trunks to capture the ambient humidity and sunlight. The greenhouse also cultivates varieties that have resulted from experimentation and hybridization. The stars of the collection are the lady's-slipper orchids: magnificent species from Southeast Asia named for their shoe-shaped lips. The other greenhouses contain ferns, bromeliads, succulents, and other tropical plants. They are open to visitors during the annual European Heritage Days, which are held in September. The garden is also home to an orchard that produces hundreds of varieties of apples, pears, and other fruits that are harvested and distributed to soup kitchens.

# A SCHOOL FOR NATURE ENTHUSIASTS

☞ The teams at the Luxembourg gardens are committed to sharing their knowledge about nature and the environment.

↠ Free classes on practice and theory are offered at the horticulture school every Tuesday and Thursday. Sign up at: jardin.senat.fr/botanique/lecoledhorticulture.html

↠ Beekeepers-in-training can take classes from the Société Centrale d'Apiculture at the Luxembourg apiary. The annual honey harvest is sold at the orangery in the fall.

↠ The gardens also host many conferences and exhibitions, and guided tours are offered every first Wednesday of the month between April and October, and every Wednesday in June.

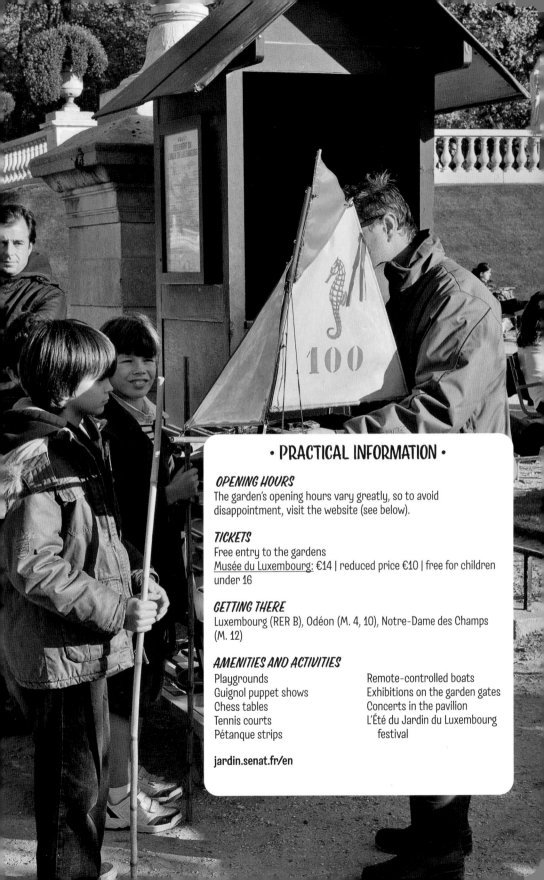

## • PRACTICAL INFORMATION •

### OPENING HOURS
The garden's opening hours vary greatly, so to avoid disappointment, visit the website (see below).

### TICKETS
Free entry to the gardens
Musée du Luxembourg: €14 | reduced price €10 | free for children under 16

### GETTING THERE
Luxembourg (RER B), Odéon (M. 4, 10), Notre-Dame des Champs (M. 12)

### AMENITIES AND ACTIVITIES
Playgrounds
Guignol puppet shows
Chess tables
Tennis courts
Pétanque strips

Remote-controlled boats
Exhibitions on the garden gates
Concerts in the pavilion
L'Été du Jardin du Luxembourg festival

jardin.senat.fr/en

# 5

# JARDIN
# du Musée Eugène-Delacroix
## Paris 6ᵉ

*This is the smallest garden featured in the book, and also probably
the most secret. Visitors are invited to immerse themselves in the private life
of the great French romantic painter Eugène Delacroix (1798–1863).
Concealed from view behind the artist's former residence,
now a museum, this several-hundred-square-foot haven
was designed by Delacroix himself.*

In 1857, Eugène Delacroix moved to 6 Rue de Furstemberg, in the Saint-Germain-des-Prés neighborhood. Jazz had not yet left its mark on the still peaceful and rather isolated area. The painter's decision was influenced by the residence's proximity to the church of Saint Sulpice, where he had been working on a monumental decorative work for several years, and by the charming little garden running along the apartments. He made it his retreat, his refuge in the city, and lived there with his housekeeper and friend, Jenny Le Guillou, up until his death. The garden is reached via a narrow wood and metal stairway leading from Delacroix's former library. The heavily

## A ROMANTIC REFUGE IN THE HEART OF SAINT-GERMAIN-DES-PRÉS

shaded paths are punctuated by several flowerbeds lined with box trees and lilyturf. Delacroix designed the garden

himself, choosing colorful or fragrant plants that would stimulate or calm his senses; the gardener Adolphe Cabot brought his ideas to life. A bill now held at the Institut National de l'Art gives an idea of the species that once flourished here: many rose bushes, including the Bengal rose; white mock oranges redolent of jasmine; lilies; climbing honeysuckle; pink or orange zinnias; nasturtiums; sunflowers, hyacinths, tulips, and more.

Currant bushes, raspberry canes, a grapevine, cherry and hazel trees, and a poplar tree, among others, completed the tableau. These bright color combinations would certainly have inspired Delacroix, whose work is distinguished by the use of pure, contrasting tones. In fact, he had his studio built directly in the garden, which today, although not identical, is very similar to the one the artist would have wandered about in. It was restored in 2012 by the gardeners Pierre Bonnaure and Sébastien Ciret using period documentation. They chose seasonal flowers and species adapted to the space, which remains in partial shade for much of the year. The garden is accessible to museum visitors, who are welcome to spend as much time as they like on the benches and small chairs scattered along the paths, and it regularly hosts events, workshops, guided tours, and artwork created by contemporary artists in homage to Delacroix. •

# The Garden of a Romantic Painter

♥ Eugène Delacroix's exceptional career left an equally exceptional legacy. When he was just 24 years old, he painted *The Barque of Dante*, a large tableau now held at the Musée du Louvre, which immediately established his reputation. Although generally associated with romanticism, he rejected this label and considered himself above all a classical painter. He was incredibly cultured and often drew inspiration from literary masterpieces such as *The Divine Comedy*, *Don Quixote*, and *Hamlet*.

But he shared many similarities with the romantics: his paintings, characterized by spectacular color contrasts, exude a unique energy and trigger strong feelings like fear or compassion. In 1832, he traveled to Morocco, where he discovered a new kind of light that deeply influenced his palette and his painting style. Internationally renowned for *Liberty Leading the People* and *The Death of Sardanapalus*, Delacroix was an artist ahead of his time who had unique ideas about color. He had many followers into the early 20th century, when fauvist artists like Henri Matisse continued to hold him up as a model.

## "THE VIEW FROM MY SMALL GARDEN AND THE CHEERFULNESS OF MY STUDIO ALWAYS GIVES ME PLEASURE."

Eugène Delacroix

# AN UNUSUAL MUSEUM

The Musée Eugène-Delacroix is unique as it is located in the very house of the artist whose work it exhibits. Today, the museum has its own collection of about 1,300 works, including paintings, lithographs, and drawings. The exhibition space is small and they cannot all be displayed at the same time, so the selection regularly changes. An exhibit dedicated to a specific aspect of Delacroix's career is held each year. The artist's home and studio were rescued in the 1920s by the Friends of Delacroix—a group of painters that included Maurice Denis and Édouard Vuillard—in homage to an artist they never knew, but whom they deeply admired. The Musée Delacroix was created in the 1950s. Today, it is managed by the Louvre and belongs to the network of "Maisons des illustres," which distinguishes buildings that preserve the cultural history of France, and hosts events and activities including concerts, guided tours, and conferences.

## • PRACTICAL INFORMATION •

**OPENING HOURS**
Wednesday to Monday: 9:30 a.m.–5:30 p.m.
Open until 9 p.m. every first Thursday of the month

**TICKETS**
Museum and garden: €9 | free for visitors under 18
and EU citizens under 26

**GETTING THERE**
Saint-Germain-des-Prés (M. 4), Mabillon (M. 10)

**AMENITIES AND ACTIVITIES**
The museum has an extensive events program that
regularly features tours, readings, concerts, workshops,
and other activities in the garden.

musee-delacroix.fr/en/

# 6

# JARDIN
# du Musée du Quai Branly
### Paris 7ᵉ

*This 4.5-acre (1.8-ha) garden is first and foremost
the manifestation of a philosophy—that of landscape designer
Gilles Clément. Designed to showcase the collections
at the Musée du Quai Branly, it is the perfect place to retreat
from the hustle and bustle of the city and unwind,
surrounded by plants from around the world.*

Located near the Eiffel Tower (which is always in view), this "global" garden invites visitors to immerse themselves in a luxuriant natural setting populated by species from various regions of the world.

Botanist and landscape designer Gilles Clément has created a kind of French-style "anti-garden" in which plants are not arranged in straight lines, but are allowed to blossom and freely interact. Here, there aren't any right angles and a large portion of the garden is left open to the unexpected. In places, the voluminous vegetation makes way for small paths that allow visitors to walk from one area to another. Each of the garden's many species are adapted to the Parisian climate. The gardeners use filtered rain water to water the plants and only use organic fertilizers. The garden at the Musée du Quai Branly is a model of environmentally sound gardening practices, where plants and birds live in harmony, and where new species regularly take up residence.

One part of the garden lies in the shadow of the museum, which is raised on pilotis (piers or pilings). The plants that live in this area, including sedge, horsetail, ferns, and spurge, can flourish without much light. They form a delicate harmony of yellows and greens that changes imperceptibly with the seasons. Several ponds bristling with bulrush provide a transitional space between the garden and the city. Ducks and marsh hens love it, and gray herons stop there on occasion. •

> *"TO MAKE A GARDEN,
> YOU NEED A PIECE
> OF LAND AND ETERNITY."*
> Gilles Clément

# A Meditative Path

Several areas inspired by Asian gardens were specially designed to provide visitors with a renewing sense of calm. To the right, upon leaving the museum, is the Candi meadow. In spring, it fills with the heady fragrance of blooming wild cherry trees, magnolias, and Japanese and Manchurian cherry trees. A little further on, the terrapin garden (named for a species of turtle) blooms in spring and summer with red valerian, which resembles the lily plant, as well as mahonia, adding a touch of yellow to the landscape. Feathery, voluminous needle grass billows along the paths. On the garden's left side, a moss garden is home to several trees, including a Wollemi pine—one of the oldest species on Earth. This area leads to a verdant theater space where performances, conferences, and events related to the world's cultures are held throughout the year.

A little further along, the rose garden offers a peaceful haven where several climbing plants—roses, of course, as well as clematis and grapevines—wind around trellises in late spring. Finally, the garden's depths hold an astonishing rounded construction designed by Jean Nouvel that makes for an ideal shelter in case of rain or blazing sun. Its roof is carpeted with a variety of plants such as stonecrop.

## A BIT OF HISTORY

The collections at the Musée du Quai Branly were assembled from those of several former ethnographic museums, where thousands of art objects from around the world were exhibited somewhat haphazardly. Until well into the 20th century, many Europeans considered these works to be the products of "primitive" peoples—exotic decorative pieces that did not merit serious study. In 1995, Jacques Chirac, an enthusiastic admirer of Asian art, expressed his wish to create a new museum dedicated to preserving, promoting, and studying art from outside of Europe. The Musée du Quai Branly, which now bears his name, was inaugurated in 2006. Its collections include masterpieces from African, Oceanian, American, and Asian artistic traditions. To house the museum, French architect Jean Nouvel designed an exceptional building that extends gracefully over a portion of the garden.

# WHY USE PILOTIS?

☞ A portion of the museum stands on 26 pilotis (piers or pilings) that evoke architecture found in Asia and the Pacific, where they are often used to keep homes above the waterline. But here they also carry out a specific function: they protect the collections from potential flooding by the nearby Seine River, and create space for plants in the garden to develop freely.

## A Tribute to Turtles

Gilles Clément wanted to pepper the garden with references to the turtle—an animal that plays a central role in many of the world's mythological traditions. A symbol of longevity and resistance, it represents, for several cultures, the foundations of the world by carrying the universe on its shell. It can be spotted in the garden's designs and amenities.

## L'Ô

♥ When night falls, what appear to be thousands of white, green, and blue fireflies emerge from among the plants. In fact, the effect is the result of an installation by Yann Kersalé, an artist who uses light to reveal an alternative side to public places after sundown. The colors selected for this work, *L'Ô* (a play on *l'eau*, French for water), evoke the different states of water: liquid, solid, and gas.

## • PRACTICAL INFORMATION •

**OPENING HOURS**
Tuesday to Sunday: 9:15 a.m.–7:30 p.m.
Thursday: 9:15 a.m.–10:15 p.m.

**TICKETS**
Free entry to the garden
Musée du Quai Branly: €12 | reduced price €9 |
free for EU citizens under 26

**GETTING THERE**
Pont de l'Alma (RER C), Alma-Marceau (M. 9), Ecole Militaire (M. 8),
Bir Hakeim (M. 6)

**AMENITIES AND ACTIVITIES**
Playgrounds            Café
Outdoor theater        Restaurant

Jardin d'Été festival in July and August: workshops, storytelling,
initiations, performances, guided walks in the garden, and
gardening workshops

quaibranly.fr/en/public-areas/the-garden

# PARC
## Monceau
### Paris 8ᵉ

*Located in the heart of the peaceful Europe neighborhood, concentrated around Place de l'Europe, Parc Monceau is a most elegant garden. Designed in 1769 at the behest of the Duke of Chartres (the future Philippe Égalité), its first owner, it was intended to surprise and enthrall aristocrats in need of a change of scenery. Even today, the many ruins found along its paths transport visitors to an idealized antiquity.*

The park is surrounded by splendid cast-iron grating decorated in places with gilded ornamentation representing various plants. Visitors entering by the main gate walk past the rotunda—a neoclassical pavilion topped with a dome and surrounded by massive columns. This imposing structure was built in the 18th century by Claude-Nicolas Ledoux. The Duke of Chartres enjoyed climbing up to the terrace,

**A GARDEN TO BE ENJOYED FOR ITS PANORAMAS.**

which used to be located where the dome is today, to admire the view. •

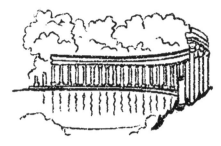

# Explore

The park was designed to reveal a series of diverse landscapes: a meadow for basking in the sun, large walkways, a water feature ideal for meditative moments, and shady, secluded paths lined with trees, many of which are very impressive. The famous Old World sycamore, near the Allée de la Comtesse-de-Ségur, has a trunk measuring 23 feet (7 m) in diameter. The park is also home to a giant ginkgo biloba, a sycamore maple, a banana tree, and a yellow poplar. In the spring, visitors can see forsythia, Japanese apple trees, and magnolias in bloom.

## LARGER-THAN-LIFE RUINS

♥ Parc Monceau's picturesque beauty owes much to the imitation ruins. The Duke of Chartres wanted to represent every time period and location in a single garden, so the park's various spaces were designed as miniature versions of the different historical universes that sparked the aristocracy's imagination or served as muses. The water feature known as a naumachia is modeled after the pools where mock naval combats were held in antiquity. In it is reflected a semicircular colonnade, taken from the funerary chapel of King Henry II, that creates an eminently poetic sight. A small bridge, similar to those spanning the canals of Venice, stretches over the brook. As for the pyramid, the obelisk, and the (empty) sarcophagus located nearby, they attest to the 18th-century taste for a largely imagined vision of ancient Egypt—hieroglyphs were not deciphered until much later, in 1822, by Jean-François Champollion.

# The Statues

S ome of the many statues scattered
throughout the park represent
mythological or allegorical figures, like a
faun or a sower. Others, dating from later
time periods, are homages to leading figures
of the 19th century, writers or composers
who left their mark on history, including
Guy de Maupassant, Alfred de Musset,
Charles Gounod, and Frédéric Chopin.
Most of the works are in neo-baroque style.
The intense expressions on the faces of
certain figures also reflect romantic lyricism.
The empty pedestals once supported bronze
statues, which were probably melted down
during World War II for their metal.

Félix Charpentier, *Young Faun* (1886).

Raoul Verlet, *Monument to Guy de Maupassant* (1897). A daydreaming young woman
representing a reader reclines at the foot of the writer's bust.

Antonin Mercié, *Monument to Alfred de Musset* or *La Nuit de Mai* (1906). The poet receives inspiration from his muse for *La Nuit de Mai*.

Jacques Froment-Meurice, *Monument to Chopin* (1906). Chopin, at the piano, is surrounded by the tearful allegories of Music and Harmony.

Léopold Bernard Bernstamm, *Monument to Édouard Pailleron* (1907). Édouard Pailleron was a poet and playwright.

Antonin Mercié, *Monument to Gounod* (1902). The composer is surrounded by characters from his operas, Sapho, Juliette, and Marguerite.

# A BIT OF HISTORY

In 1769, at the request of the Duke of Chartres, the garden designer Louis Carrogis Carmontelle created a garden of English and Chinese influence. He skillfully combined imitations of untamed nature—characteristic of English gardens—with more Asian features. The park was, above all, a *folie*: a term used to describe high society whimsy in matters of architecture or garden design. After the French Revolution, the land was seized by the state. The park in its current form was entirely redesigned during the Second Empire, although a few original elements remain.

*A View of Turkish Tents from Parc Monceau.* Engraving by Jean-Baptiste Delafosse after Carmontelle (1779).

The Duke of Chartres's garden contained many *fabriques*: small buildings without any real function that served primarily to compose landscapes resembling paintings. Scattered pell-mell throughout the park were a Chinese pagoda, a farm, several windmills, a medievalesque tower, a minaret, Greco-Roman-style temples, and striped Turkish tents.

## • PRACTICAL INFORMATION •

### OPENING HOURS
<u>Summer</u>: Open daily 7 a.m.–10 p.m.
<u>September</u>: Open daily 7 a.m.–9 p.m.
<u>Winter</u>: Open daily 7 a.m.–8 p.m.

### TICKETS
Free entry

### GETTING THERE
Monceau (M. 2), Malesherbes (M. 3)

### AMENITIES AND ACTIVITIES
Free guided tours organized by the city's Parks
and Gardens department
Playgrounds; refreshment stand

paris.fr/lieux/parc-monceau-1804 (in French)

# PARC
# Floral
## Paris 12ᵉ

*Extending over 77 acres (31 ha), this is one of the largest parks in Paris, home to a dizzying variety of trees, flowers, bushes, birds, and small animals. Parc Floral is a veritable nature conservatory where botany enthusiasts will find many sources of inspiration for their gardens.*

P arc Floral comprises many spaces that showcase more than 7,500 plant varieties. Sustainable management practices have allowed biodiversity to gradually reclaim the various landscapes that have been recreated in the park. The central reflecting pool is surrounded by a vale of flowers—a floral tapestry that blooms with a thousand colors depending on the time of year. Various approaches to the garden enable visitors to discover the park at its finest in every season: a large pine forest; an aquatic garden, where water lilies and lotuses flower in the summer; a "four-seasons" garden; an unusual garden that is home to strange plants and forgotten vegetables; a small garden where children can learn to protect nature while having fun; an alpine garden; and collections of irises, geraniums, dahlias, and more. The various exhibition pavilions are home to microclimates where rare species like

**FLOWERS ARE EVERYWHERE, PROVIDING AN IDEAL PLACE TO WANDER.**

impressive bonsais are cultivated. Visitors can stroll endlessly around this magnificent park.

Parc Floral was also designed with relaxation and culture in mind: there are large playgrounds, mini-golf, and spaces for theater and music. It also hosts events like the Paris Jazz Festival, Classique au Vert, and Les Pestacles for children. •

# The Dahlia Collection and the International Competition

*Parc Floral is proud of its many flower collections that include irises, tulips, hydrangeas, and geraniums.*

The dahlia collection is probably the most remarkable of all. It includes more than 420 varieties, making it one of the largest in Europe. Since the 18th century, horticulturalists have experimented with and crossbred these flowers, which are native to Mexico and Colombia, resulting in an infinite variety of forms and colors: pompon dahlias, ball-shaped dahlias, dwarf dahlias, cactus dahlias, lace dahlias—the list goes on.

These magnificent flowers grow in a garden near the pine forest, where they bloom from August to November. As winter approaches, the tubers are dug up and placed in storage until the following spring.

Parc Floral is known worldwide for its international dahlia competition, held in August or September. It is well worth attending: the dahlias are in full bloom and visitors are invited to select three winners each year.

# A BIT OF HISTORY

Created between 1967 and 1969 on former military grounds to host a temporary horticulture exhibition, Parc Floral was designed by the landscape architect Daniel Collin. He wanted to offer Parisians a space that "could meet the needs of an ever-growing number of people who want to get closer to nature to partake of its joys."

The exhibition pavilions are strongly inspired by Japanese architecture, which was fashionable after the 1964 Tokyo Olympic Games. This same spirit is found throughout the park, such as in the aquatic garden, which is replete with water lilies and lotuses in summer, and the Japanese garden, home to a bamboo grove.

# Bloom Calendar

| | |
|---|---|
| Camellia | December ⇢ April |
| Dahlia | August ⇢ November |
| Perennial geranium | Mid-April ⇢ December |
| Iris | May ⇢ late June |
| Medicinal plant garden | April ⇢ late October |
| Magnolia | March, April, and June ⇢ October |
| Geranium, South African plants | June ⇢ late October |
| Peony | Mid-April ⇢ mid-June |
| Rhododendron | Mid-March ⇢ mid-July |
| Bulbs and tulips | Mid-March ⇢ mid-June |

## THE PATH OF EVOLUTION: THE LONG HISTORY OF PLANTS

The "path of evolution" is a one-of-a-kind garden that illustrates the way in which plants have adapted to changes in climate over the last 500 million years. Each meter of the path represents a million years: ferns, algae, and horsetails—the first plants to appear on Earth—give way to flowering plants, for a total of more than 600 different species.

# The Pine Forest

The great pine forest, which occupies nearly 7.5 acres (3 ha), is much older than the rest of the park. This calm space frequented by squirrels is home to black pine and Scots pine; in spring, rhododendrons, azaleas, magnolias, and camellias bloom here, as well as a collection of false goat's beard in June and July.

# Jardin Botanique de Paris

....................................

*Parc Floral, along with Parc de Bagatelle, the Auteuil greenhouses, and the Paris arboretum, belongs to the Paris Botanical Gardens: a group of gardens devoted to the study and conservation of plants.*

....................................

These four parks are home to a total of more than 15,000 plant species, including some that are at risk of extinction. Each of them has received Jardin Remarquable status from the Ministry of Culture. The parks in the Paris Botanical Gardens are committed to informing the general public about the importance of biodiversity and its conservation. At Parc Floral, the Maison Paris Nature offers many nature-related activities—including a walk that takes visitors around beehives, insect houses, living walls, an uncultivated plot, and a pond—and has many resources to learn more about the flora and fauna.

## THE BUTTERFLY GARDEN

The Maison Paris Nature includes a greenhouse where butterflies freely flutter about. It is open to visitors Wednesday to Friday and on Sunday, from mid-May to mid-October.

# A HAVEN FOR BIRDS

Parc Floral is a natural oasis, and the birds know it: some live here year-round, while others stop in from time to time. Kinglets, tits, warblers, woodpeckers, jays, greenfinches, robins, swallows, moorhens, tawny owls, shelducks, and geese find everything they need to survive in this park.

Lucky visitors will spot falcons perching on the Château de Vincennes. Keep an eye open for the peacocks that live in the garden. It should be easy to spot them—they just love parading about.

## Sculptures of Stone and Flowers

Several contemporary sculptures are scattered throughout the park, including a monumental fountain by François Stahly made of large blocks of black granite, and Oleg Goudcoff's *À cœur ouvert* (Open heart)—an intriguing sculpture that resembles a split tree trunk. Extraordinary floral compositions are often presented during competitions and other events.

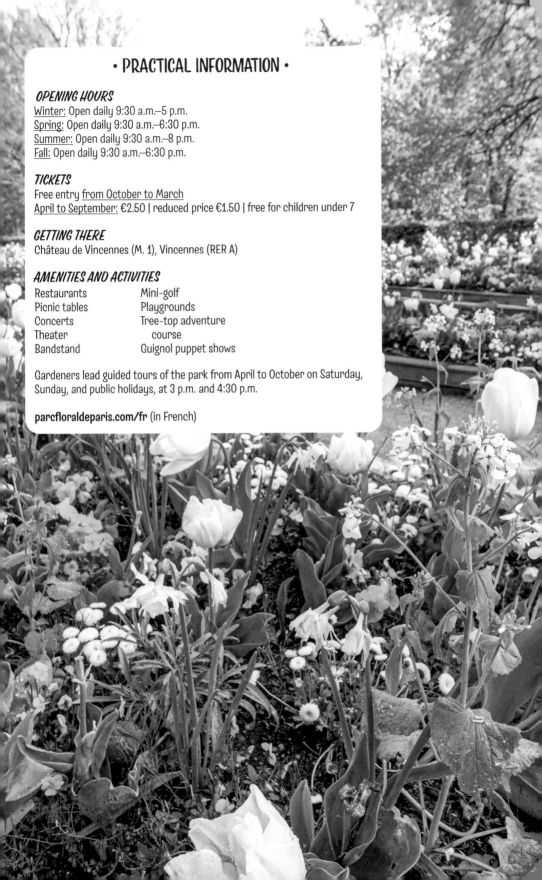

# • PRACTICAL INFORMATION •

## OPENING HOURS
<u>Winter:</u> Open daily 9:30 a.m.–5 p.m.
<u>Spring:</u> Open daily 9:30 a.m.–6:30 p.m.
<u>Summer:</u> Open daily 9:30 a.m.–8 p.m.
<u>Fall:</u> Open daily 9:30 a.m.–6:30 p.m.

## TICKETS
Free entry <u>from October to March</u>
<u>April to September:</u> €2.50 | reduced price €1.50 | free for children under 7

## GETTING THERE
Château de Vincennes (M. 1), Vincennes (RER A)

## AMENITIES AND ACTIVITIES

| | |
|---|---|
| Restaurants | Mini-golf |
| Picnic tables | Playgrounds |
| Concerts | Tree-top adventure |
| Theater | course |
| Bandstand | Guignol puppet shows |

Gardeners lead guided tours of the park from April to October on Saturday, Sunday, and public holidays, at 3 p.m. and 4:30 p.m.

parcfloraldeparis.com/fr (in French)

# JARDINS & ARBORETUM de l'École du Breuil

## Paris 8ᵉ

*This is no ordinary garden. Here, visitors may cross paths with gardeners-in-training taking a class or engaged in practical work. The École du Breuil is, above all, a teaching center where students can deepen their knowledge thanks to what is essentially an open–air encyclopedia—the 57-acre (23-ha) garden, open to the public since 2013, is home to more than 10,000 plant varieties.*

## SO MUCH MORE THAN JUST A SCHOOL.

The École Théorique et Pratique d'Arboriculture de la Ville de Paris was founded in 1867 on Baron Haussmann's initiative. During the second half of the 19th century, Haussmann carried out a series of large public works projects that would forever change the city's appearance. At the same time, Emperor Napoleon III established vast parks to enable Parisians in every neighborhood to unwind and breathe air made fresher by vegetation. The engineer Jean-Charles Adolphe Alphand was tasked with overseeing the construction of four parks located at the city's cardinal points: Bois de Boulogne to the west, Parc des Buttes-Chaumont to the north, Parc Montsouris to the south, and Bois de Vincennes to the east. A large number of new gardeners had to be trained to maintain them. Empress Eugénie suggested creating a school where they could learn to care for plants and design landscapes by directly observing nature.

The first school was built in the town of Saint-Mandé; it had two fruit gardens, an orchard, a vineyard, thickets, and a nursery. In the 1930s, to make room for the Palais de la Porte-Dorée, the establishment was moved to Bois de Vincennes, and the plant collection was expanded.

Many new spaces were added over time, including a rose garden, a vegetable garden, several orchards, greenhouses, an English garden, a fruticetum containing shrubs, and a huge 32-acre (13-ha) arboretum.

Today, the school—now named for Alphonse du Breuil, one of its first directors—enrolls many students, as well as people making a career change and hobby gardeners. Protecting the environment holds a central place in the school's curriculum, which addresses issues that have become imperatives, such as using local plants and permaculture techniques, and collecting rain water. Access to the park, which obtained Jardin Remarquable status in 2014, is free. •

jardin remarquable

## MIXED BORDERS

➳ Near the entrance to the garden, visitors can stroll among mixed borders composed of various perennials, annuals, and shrubs. This principle, updated by landscape designer Gertrude Jekyll in the early 20th century, is based on combining plants according to their characteristics and colors. The borders form carpets of greenery overflowing with life that offer plenty of inspiration for home gardeners. The plant collection includes iris, carnation, geranium, forget-me-not, foxglove, daisy, grasses, spurge, clematis, silvergrass, mimosa, and Barbary fig.

## THE ROCK GARDEN

➳ The rock garden is a pleasant space where nature blossoms freely. The landscape, which includes rock walls, winding paths, brooks, and a wooden bridge, evokes both the mountains and Japan. A stroll through the garden feels like an escape from the city. The plant collection includes carnation, geranium, hellebore, bulbous plants (hyacinths, tulips), anemone, primrose, musk adox, sweet woodruff, aromatic plants (thyme, oregano, savory), ferns, Japanese maple, hornbeam, and holm oak.

# JARDIN PAYSAGER

➻ Modeled after English garden design principles, this space is full of surprises, including sprawling lawns, wooded areas, beds of heather, and bamboo. A pond completes the bucolic setting. The plant collection includes peony, bulbous plants (narcissus, crocus, morning glory), azalea, rhododendron, hydrangea, camellia, giant Brazilian rhubarb, magnolia, maple, purple beech, bald cypress, Japanese plane tree, Chinese parasol, weeping ash, ginkgo biloba, and horse chestnut.

# THE ROSE GARDEN

➻ The rose garden stretches out in front of the school's main building. A harmonious combination of French garden design and art deco style, it comprises regularly spaced beds of roses arranged around a rectangular pool inhabited by carp and surrounded by six palm trees. Climbing roses wind around a delightful arbor. The plant collection includes rose bushes, ground-cover roses, climbing roses, and tree roses.

## THE ARBORETUM

☞ The arboretum is a 32-acre (13-ha) wood adjoining the gardens. It was designed to teach students at the École du Breuil to recognize and care for trees native to France, as well as species from more distant regions. Today, it forms part of the Paris Botanical Gardens, along with Parc Floral, the Auteuil greenhouse gardens, and Parc de Bagatelle. The trees are organized by family, including conifers with needles or scales, maple, linden, oak, willow, and Lebanese cedar.

➻ The arboretum is home to several remarkable trees, including examples of the Chinese hazel, Chinese tulip tree, American chestnut, handkerchief tree, Caucasian elm, weeping pear, metasequoia, and Korean pine.

## THE FRUTICETUM

A fruticetum is a shrub garden. The word comes from the Latin *frutex*, which means "small tree." The École du Breuil's collection of more than 900 different species form tableaux whose colors change with the seasons. The plant collection includes spindle, dogwood, chimonanthe, honeysuckle, poliothyrsis, and Mexican orange tree.

## VEGETABLE GARDEN, ORCHARDS, AND GREENHOUSES

➻ In the walled vegetable garden and in the two orchards, vegetables, flowers, bushes, and fruit trees are cultivated using sustainable methods. Students learn to master a wide range of traditional and modern techniques.

➻ Some areas of the gardens at the École du Breuil are not usually open to the public, but can be discovered during events or classes.

➻ The greenhouses are home to plants that require protection from the cold, such as tropical or Mediterranean varieties, succulents, and cacti.

## Classes for Home Gardeners

♥ The school offers both theoretical and hands-on classes in French for home gardeners who would like professional advice about garden design, or to learn more about plants and acquire new gardening skills.

☞ For more information: ecoledubreuil.fr/adultes/coursde-jardinage-permaculture/

## • PRACTICAL INFORMATION •

### OPENING HOURS
April 1 to September 30: 9 a.m.–7 p.m.
October and March: 9 a.m.–6 p.m.
November 1 to February 28: 9 a.m.–5 p.m.

### TICKETS
Free entry

### GETTING THERE
Joinville-Le-Pont (RER A), or Château de Vincennes
(M. 1), then bus 112 to Carrefour de Beauté

### AMENITIES AND ACTIVITIES
Free guided tours and activities during the Fête de
L'École du Breuil (May), and European Heritage Days
and the Fête des Jardins (September).

**ecoledubreuil.fr/jardin/** (in French)

# 10

# PARC
# Montsouris
### Paris 14ᵉ

*It is a pleasure to walk through this sweeping park in any season.
Designed to be a southern equivalent of Parc des Buttes-Chaumont
to the north, it includes a large artificial lake surrounded by shaded areas
and vast glades. In the words of Agnès Varda, Parc Montsouris
is an astonishing "imitation of nature in the midst of nature."*

D uring the second half of the 19th century, under the reign of Napoleon III, Baron Haussmann undertook significant public works projects that completely changed the face of the city. By cutting wide avenues through the capital, he hoped to slow the epidemics caused by overcrowding, as well as fight crime, which thrived in the dim, narrow alleyways. He spearheaded his project with the construction of parks at the city's four cardinal points: Parc des Buttes-Chaumont to the north, Bois de Boulogne to the west, Bois de Vincennes to the east, and Parc Montsouris to the south. At the time, it was believed that parks prevented disease from spreading.

**FIVE CENTURIES OF HISTORY BLEND HARMONIOUSLY IN THIS COMPLEX LANDSCAPE.**

Parc Montsouris is located on a site formerly occupied by dark and gloomy quarries. The engineer Jean-Charles Adolphe Alphand was tasked

with building the park, which was no easy feat due to the uneven terrain and the catacombs tunneling underground. But the construction of Parc des Buttes-Chaumont, which he had overseen several years earlier, had proven to be a far greater undertaking.

☞ Working with landscape designer Jean-Pierre Barillet-Deschamps, Alphand designed a park that was inspired by London gardens. He had an artificial lake, fed by an aqueduct, dug, and landscaped imitations of natural features—including prairies, glades, waterfalls, thickets, woods, and bridges—were created around this central water feature.

☞ Several rustic pavilions give the ensemble a picturesque charm. It can be difficult to tell fact from fiction here: for example, most of the "wooden" fences lining the paths are actually made of concrete. Parc Montsouris was inaugurated in 1869 and opened to visitors from around the world during the 1878 World's Fair. Today, it continues to be an immensely popular place for Parisians who are weary of the bustle of city life to rest and recharge. •

## THE NAME "PARC MONTSOURIS"

☞ *Montsouris* is derived from the nickname *Moc Souris* or *Moque Souris*, meaning "mouse mocker"—a reference to the many grain windmills that once lined the Bièvre River, which used to pass nearby.

> *"PARC MONTSOURIS IS THE PLACE*
> *WHERE I TAKE MY ODDITIES FOR A WALK*
> *WHERE I SCRUB MY ANTENNAE CLEAN*
> *OF THE MEANNESS OF LIFE."*
>
> Jacques Higelin

## PAVILLON MONTSOURIS

☞ What could be nicer after a long walk than relaxing in the Pavillon Montsouris? Featuring a red-and-yellow striped brick facade adorned with ceramic ornamentation, this restaurant was created in 1889 and has hosted some exceptional guests, including Lenin and Trotsky, Simone de Beauvoir, and Jean-Paul Sartre. You'll need a certain budget to have lunch here, though.

772 - PARIS (14') - Parc de Montsouris - Le Bardo
Reproducteon du Palais du Bey de Tunis (Exposition de 1867), devenu l'Observatoire météorologique de Montsouris J.H.

## The Weather Station

♥ Parc Montsouris is home to a weather station that has been in operation since April 1872. The observatory used to be housed in an astonishing palace of Hispano-Moorish style modeled after a residence of the bey of Tunis. That building was destroyed in a mysterious fire in 1991. The station has one of the oldest databases in France, thanks to which we know that the lowest temperature ever recorded in the capital was -11°F (-23.9°C), in 1879. As for the highest temperature, the 1947 record of 104.7°F (40.4°C) has been exceeded several times since 2019. Luckily, parks and gardens provide the city's inhabitants with a bit of coolness in summer.

## 1,400 TREES

☞ Near the lake, a majestic gingko biloba stands nearly 89 feet (27 m) tall. It is recognizable by its fan-shaped leaves that look like duck's feet and its fruit resembling small mirabelle plums—but careful, they are not edible! On the opposite bank, a sinuous oak with intertwining branches bends over the water. Near the weather station, on the park's higher ground, stand a giant sequoia and a Caucasian wingnut—a decorative tree that blooms with lovely garlands of green flowers from June. The city of Paris has put together a walking tour specially designed for tree lovers that features plane, oak, beech, cedar, and maple.

⤷ paris.fr/pages/parcours-au-parc-montsouris-4020 (in French)

# Statues

Parc Montsouris stands out for its numerous hidden treasures. In addition to picturesque bridges and architecture, the park is home to many intriguing statues by artists such as Henry Bouchard, Jules Felix Coutan, and Edmond Desca, who created the fascinating *Death of a Lion* in 1912.

Jules Coutan, *Column of Armed Peace* (1888). "If you want peace, prepare for war," this allegory seems to say.

Edmond Desca, *Death of a Lion* (1912).
This dead lion, carried by three men, is heart-wrenchingly realistic.

René Baucour, *First Shiver* (1909).

*La Mire du Sud* (1806).
This monument was intended
to mark the Paris meridian, but it was
not placed on the right spot.

Morice Lipsi, *Bathers* (1946).

Costa Valsenis, *Purity* (1955).

# The Park's Residents

..............................................

*Parc Montsouris is a refuge
for many animal species.*

..............................................

Birds appreciate its artificial lake (mallards, both black and white swans, geese, moorhens, coots, bar-headed geese), as well as its tall trees (nuthatches, green woodpeckers, oak jays, ring-necked parakeets, house wrens, great crested tits).

Lucky visitors may even spot hawks, but they are very discreet. The lake is inhabited by fish such as koi, bream, sun perch, and pike-perch. And small mammals like bats, squirrels, and hedgehogs find the calm and food they need to survive here.

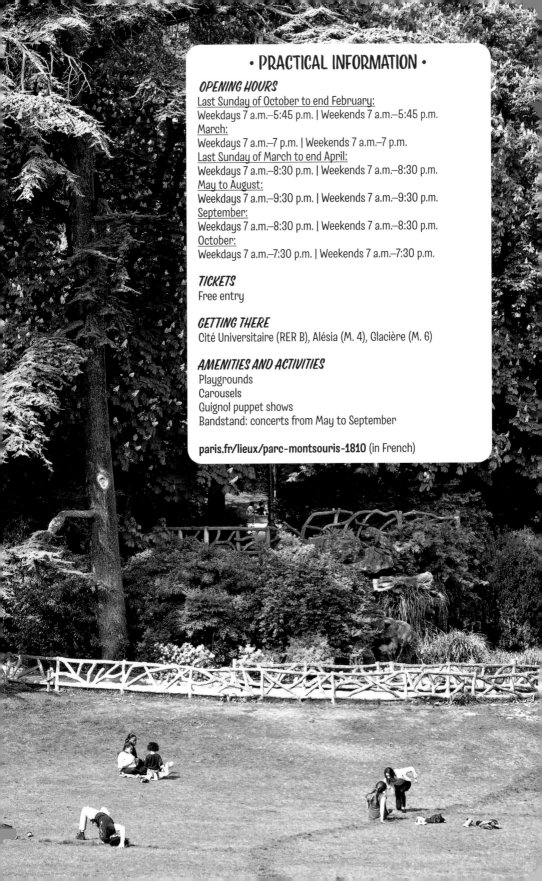

# • PRACTICAL INFORMATION •

### OPENING HOURS
<u>Last Sunday of October to end February:</u>
Weekdays 7 a.m.–5:45 p.m. | Weekends 7 a.m.–5:45 p.m.
<u>March:</u>
Weekdays 7 a.m.–7 p.m. | Weekends 7 a.m.–7 p.m.
<u>Last Sunday of March to end April:</u>
Weekdays 7 a.m.–8:30 p.m. | Weekends 7 a.m.–8:30 p.m.
<u>May to August:</u>
Weekdays 7 a.m.–9:30 p.m. | Weekends 7 a.m.–9:30 p.m.
<u>September:</u>
Weekdays 7 a.m.–8:30 p.m. | Weekends 7 a.m.–8:30 p.m.
<u>October:</u>
Weekdays 7 a.m.–7:30 p.m. | Weekends 7 a.m.–7:30 p.m.

### TICKETS
Free entry

### GETTING THERE
Cité Universitaire (RER B), Alésia (M. 4), Glacière (M. 6)

### AMENITIES AND ACTIVITIES
Playgrounds
Carousels
Guignol puppet shows
Bandstand: concerts from May to September

**paris.fr/lieux/parc-montsouris-1810** (in French)

# 11

# PARC
## André-Citroën
### Paris 15ᵉ

*Parc André-Citroën was built by a collective of architects
and landscape designers on the site of a former automobile factory.
Today, this huge park blends perfectly into its modern surroundings.
In addition to a gigantic central lawn and a splash pad, which provides welcome
coolness in summer, it has several hidden themed gardens where plant species
are grouped according to color and symbolic meaning—a must-see curiosity.*

For several centuries, the history of the Javel neighborhood has been closely tied to advances in science and industry. Starting in the late 18th century, chemical products were made there, including bleach, which to this day is still called *eau de Javel* in French—"Javel water." During World War I, André Citroën built a munitions factory on the site of the present-day park. The employees were primarily women: essential to the war effort, they were nicknamed *munitionettes*. The building was later transformed into a prosperous

**THIS DECIDEDLY CONTEMPORARY PARK IS ONE OF THE MOST RECENT IN PARIS, AND THE ONLY ONE WITH A VIEW OVER THE SEINE.**

automobile factory that produced, among other models, the famous Citroën DS.

In 1979, the city of Paris bought the land with the intention of creating a leisure space for locals. Architects Patrick Berger, Jean-Paul Viguier, and Jean-

François Jodry, and landscape designers Allain Provost and Gilles Clément (who designed the garden at the Musée du Quai Branly) were tasked with conceiving a gigantic park that would harmoniously combine nature and architecture, as well as wide-open views and other hidden spaces.

The large central lawn, where Parisians gather in summer, is similar to those in other parks in the capital, such as the Tuileries or the Champ-de-Mars. Bordered with grasses, sculpted bushes, and trees, this huge green rectangle is traversed by canals and dotted with fountains, and opens directly onto the Seine. A little further on, a splash pad provides refreshing coolness during heatwaves.

Here, children rule. Large playgrounds were built for them in the white garden and the black garden, whose names refer to the colors of the species planted in each one: the first is home to silvery perennials like anemone and candytuft; the second to black iris, purple rose, rhododendron, pine, and other dark vegetation.

Parc André-Citroën brings together in a single location monumental, almost

futuristic landscapes and smaller spaces where nature is allowed to develop freely and evolve with the seasons.

This contrast makes it a unique place that offers a lifetime's worth of exploration. •

# Serial Gardens

Located on the park's north side, these six small gardens form a miniature cosmos. Each one features a variety of plants related to a color, a metal, a sense, a celestial body or planet, and a day. Home gardeners will find a wealth of inspiration here.

| | | | | | |
|---|---|---|---|---|---|
| **Jardin bleu** (Blue Garden) | Copper | Smell | Venus | Friday | Laburnum<br>Blue blossom<br>Blue sage<br>Veronica |
| **Jardin vert** (Green Garden) | Pewter | Hearing | Jupiter | Thursday | Maple<br>Oak<br>Rhubarb<br>Angelica |
| **Jardin orange** (Orange Garden) | Mercury | Touch | Mercury | Wednesday | False cypress<br>Golden-rain tree<br>Azalea<br>Foxtail lily |
| **Jardin rouge** (Red Garden) | Iron | Taste | Mars | Tuesday | Cherry<br>Mulberry<br>Holly<br>Poppy |
| **Jardin argenté** (Silver Garden) | Silver | Sight | Moon | Monday | Thistle<br>Santolina<br>Oat<br>Wormwood |
| **Jardin doré** (Gold Garden) | Gold | Sixth sense | Sun | Sunday | Black locust<br>Hazel<br>Mock orange<br>Gold spirea |

# JARDIN EN MOUVEMENT

♥ Here, nature has regained its rightful place. Gilles Clément designed this garden according to a distinctive philosophy that calls for letting plants interact and for interfering as little as possible with the landscape. The area now resembles uncultivated land, and wild plants like foxglove, poppy, and balsam can be found.

# The Greenhouses

👉 The park's east entrance is flanked by two large greenhouses measuring 49 feet (15 m) in height, with entirely transparent walls that reveal the plants within. The first one houses an orangery and the second is home to plants from hot climates.

## FLOAT ABOVE PARIS

♥ When weather conditions are right, the Paris hot air balloon is one of the park's must-see attractions. It regularly takes 30 people on an unforgettable ride 492 feet (150 m) above the ground.

☛ From that height, the view of the city is stunning. And there is no risk of flying too high: the balloon is firmly attached to the ground by a cable.

☛ The helium balloon is also used to measure the quality of the city's air.

# • PRACTICAL INFORMATION •

## OPENING HOURS

Last Sunday of October to end February:
Weekdays 8 a.m.–5:45 p.m. | Weekends 9 a.m.–5:45 p.m.
March: Weekdays 8 a.m.–7 p.m. | Weekends 9 a.m.–7 p.m.
Last Sunday of March to end April:
Weekdays 8 a.m.–8:30 p.m. | Weekends 9 am–8:30 p.m.
May to August:
Weekdays 8 a.m.–9:30 p.m. | Weekends 9 a.m.–9:30 p.m.
September:
Weekdays 8 am–8:30 p.m. | Weekend 9 a.m.–8:30 p.m.
October:
Weekdays 8 a.m.–7:30 p.m. | Weekend 9 a.m.–7:30 p.m.

## TICKETS

Free entry
Paris hot air balloon: 12 and over €18 | 3–11 €12 |
free for children under 3

## GETTING THERE

Lourmel (M. 8),  Javel – André Citroën (M. 10), Pont du
Garigliano - Hôpital Européen Georges Pompidou (RER C)

## AMENITIES AND ACTIVITIES

| | |
|---|---|
| Playgrounds | Refreshment stand |
| Picnic tables | Carousels |

paris.fr/lieux/parc-andre-citroen-1791 (in French)

# 12

# BOIS
# de Boulogne
## Paris 16ᵉ

*Bois de Boulogne is known for its large clearings,
gourmet restaurants, and elite sports clubs. But hidden within
this huge green space with a surface area of more
than 2,000 acres (800 ha)—twice the size of NYC's Central Park—
are less frequented areas that are home to some remarkable plants.*

## A GREAT PLACE TO GET LOST.

Adjoining Paris's very chic 16th arrondissement, Bois de Boulogne is a vast park where *le Tout-Paris* gathers, especially when summer comes around. It is the perfect place for long walks, as well as a host of outdoor activities including cycling, tennis, and horseback riding. In fact, the park is home to several high-profile sporting complexes including the Longchamp and Auteuil racetracks and the Roland-Garros stadium.

Centuries ago, the kings of France relaxed here by organizing large hunting parties. In the 7th century, when Dagobert ruled the Franks, there were even bears to be found. Bois de Boulogne was opened to the public in the 18th century under Louis XVI. Over time, it became a meeting place for the aristocracy, then for the bourgeoisie: mondaine and demimondaine ladies regularly rode through the park on horseback or in their carriages, hoping to be admired by passersby.

Bois de Boulogne was completely transformed under the reign of Napoleon III. The engineer Jean-Charles Adolphe Alphand (who later oversaw the construction of Parc des Buttes-Chaumont) and the landscape designer Jean-Pierre Barillet-Deschamps remodeled it into the park we know today. Two artificial lakes were dug, along with a small brook and several ponds. Architect Gabriel Davioud designed various pavilions and other structures to enliven the landscape. Despite these massive works, nature has taken over in various areas of the park: fish and frogs are abundant in the lakes and ponds, and many forest species have taken up residence in the undergrowth. •

## A STORYBOOK SETTING

♥ Those who have never been to Bois de Boulogne have probably seen it in a painting or read about it in a book. The park has inspired history's greatest artists, and 19th-century French literature is full of innumerable walks in the "Bois."

☞ Impressionist painters such as Berthe Morisot and Auguste Renoir greatly appreciated this park that allowed them access to a bit of nature near the city. A nine-year-old Marcel Proust had his first asthma attack just after visiting the park, and Simone de Beauvoir liked to wander its paths when she was a young girl.

Alfred de Dreux, *Mademoiselle de Mossellmann Riding
in Bois de Boulogne,* oil on canvas (1848).

# The Auteuil Greenhouse Gardens

········································

*The greenhouse gardens
are located near the south entrance.*

········································

Arranged around a French-style flowerbed, five greenhouses—sophisticated sculptures in glass and cast iron—house rare plants from around the world. There is also a palmerium measuring nearly 53 feet (16 m) in height and a charming aviary. The buildings' architecture is typical of the late 19th century, a period that witnessed the emergence of a genuine passion for exotic plants and conservatories throughout Europe.

❦ Various microclimates have been recreated inside these small plant museums. In the tropical greenhouse, the ambient humidity and heat create ideal conditions for species such as traveler's palm (with elegant fan-shaped foliage), and kapok, banana, and papaya trees. This greenhouse is also home to orchids, which, in tropical forests, usually attach themselves to trees in order to capture sunlight and humidity in the air.

❦ Another greenhouse holds astonishing plants that grow in New Caledonia, a remote archipelago in the Pacific Ocean. Most of them are endemic species: the particular characteristics they have developed to adapt to their habitat make them unlike any others. Many of them are at risk of extinction.

❦ The greenhouses also contain plants from the Sahel region, which are characterized by their resistance to drought, such as cacti and other succulents, and ficus. Growing alongside these species that have evolved to withstand their habitat are horticultural plants—the result of experimentation and hybridization, usually for decorative ends. Recently, six new greenhouses were built, in which ecosystems found in Africa, South America, Southeast Asia, and Australia have been recreated.

jardin
remarquable

🕯 Today, along with Parc de Bagatelle (which is also located in Bois de Boulogne), Parc Floral, and the Paris arboretum, the Auteuil greenhouses form the Paris Botanical Gardens: a group of gardens created to study and protect a plant collection containing more than 15,000 species. It has also been granted Jardin Remarquable status.

## THE NAME "BOIS DE BOULOGNE"

☞ In the early 14th century, Philip the Fair (Philip IV of France) traveled to Boulogne-sur-Mer, located in the present-day Pas-de-Calais *département*, for the marriage of his daughter, Isabelle, to Edward II of England. At the time, the city was a major pilgrimage site. The French king wanted to create an equivalent near Paris, and he had a church dedicated to the Virgin Mary built in the village of Menus-lez-Saint-Cloud. Called Notre-Dame-de-Boulogne-la-Petite, the church gave its name to the town Boulogne-Billancourt, where it is located today—and to the woods, Bois de Boulogne.

## THÉÂTRE DE VERDURE

In the Pré-Catelan, an open-air green theater was built among several themed gardens inspired by Shakespeare plays: *Hamlet, The Tempest, A Midsummer Night's Dream, Macbeth,* and *As You Like It.* In summer, actors take over this original setting to present new productions and reinterpretations of famous works.

# Majestic Trees

*In Bois de Boulogne, the oak is king, accounting for around 35 percent of the trees present. But visitors wandering through the park will encounter many other species that are remarkable for their beauty, stature, or age.*

♥ In the Pré-Catelan garden, in the heart of the woods, a magnolia flowers every summer. A venerable sequoia planted in 1872 also grows here, as well as an araucaria, or monkey puzzle tree, so named for its pointy leaves. A large artificial waterfall constructed with rocks that give it a natural appearance cascades nearby; created under Napoleon III, it is sometimes turned off to save water. A Lebanese cedar and a bald cypress rise above the adjacent water feature.

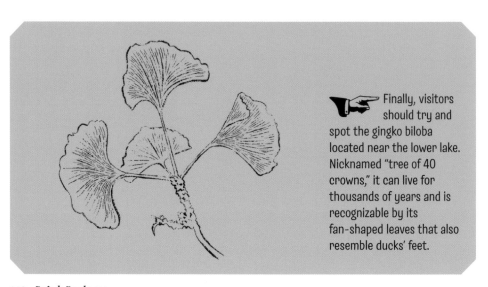

☞ Finally, visitors should try and spot the gingko biloba located near the lower lake. Nicknamed "tree of 40 crowns," it can live for thousands of years and is recognizable by its fan-shaped leaves that also resemble ducks' feet.

## FONDATION LOUIS VUITTON

Aerial views of Bois de Boulogne show an impressive structure distinctly standing out against the trees: the Fondation Louis Vuitton, built under the direction of world-renowned architect Frank Gehry, was inaugurated in 2014.

→ Fans of modern and contemporary art will appreciate its events program: the museum's ambitious exhibitions present exceptional works that may not be on view anywhere else.

343 Paris. Jardin d' Acclimatation: le Palmarium.

## JARDIN D'ACCLIMATATION

→ Opened in 1860, the Jardin d'Acclimatation is the oldest theme park in the capital still in operation. Although today it is a pleasant location for leisure activities, its dark past should not be forgotten: it was not all that long ago that it hosted human zoos, especially during large colonial exhibitions.

# • PRACTICAL INFORMATION •

### OPENING HOURS
Open daily, 24h
However, it is not advisable to walk in the park late at night.

### TICKETS
Free entry to the park and Auteuil greenhouses
Entrance to the Jardin d'Acclimatation varies according to the
day and attractions, and is free for children shorter than
2 ft. 7½ in. (80 cm)
Fondation Louis Vuitton: €16 | reduced price €10 | under 18s €5

### GETTING THERE
Avenue Foch (RER C), Porte Dauphine (M. 2), Rue de la Pompe
(M. 9), Michel-Ange – Auteuil (M. 9, 10)

### AMENITIES AND ACTIVITIES
Playgrounds
Bike paths
Picnic tables
Theater
Restaurants:  L'Auberge du Bonheur, Le Chalet des Îles,
    Les Jardins de Bagatelle, La Grande Cascade (✿),
    Le Pré Catelan (✿✿✿)
No swimming allowed.

paris.fr/lieux/bois-de-boulogne-2779 (in French)

# 13

# PARC
## de Bagatelle
### Paris 16ᵉ

*The timeless Parc de Bagatelle is located north of Bois de Boulogne. Some consider it to be the most beautiful garden in the capital, but the jury is still out. However, its rose garden and history certainly make it the most unique garden in western Paris.*

What is now Parc de Bagatelle was once the site of a lodge that was used during royal hunting parties. In the 18th century, during the reign of Louis XV, it was purchased by Marechal d'Estrées and became popular with libertines:

### A FOLIE FOR THE COUNT OF ARTOIS.

members of the nobility indulged in frivolous leisure at extravagant parties held in this lush setting hidden from view. In 1775, the Count of Artois, Louis XVI's brother and the future King Charles X, acquired it. Two years later, Queen Marie Antoinette set him the incredible challenge of building a new residence there in less than 100 days. In the end, he succeeded in just 64 days with the help of architect François-Joseph Bélanger and 900 laborers. The Château de Bagatelle is the epitome of a *folie*—a type of small building that wealthy aristocrats built on a whim, with no regard for cost. The estate went through several different owners who enlarged the château, expanded the gardens, and built an orangery. It was purchased by the city in the early 20th century. After years of neglect, the estate was restored and remodeled by Jean-Claude-Nicolas Forestier, custodian of Bois de Boulogne, who turned it into the delightful botanical garden that welcomes visitors today. He also created the large rose garden, which is famous among flower enthusiasts throughout Europe. •

# The Rose Garden

The rose garden in Parc de Bagatelle is one of the largest and most beautiful of its kind in France, with more than 1,200 varieties spread over 4 acres (1.6 ha). Established in 1905 by Jean-Claude-Nicolas Forestier, the garden continues to evolve, year after year. Originally, the flowers were largely presented in uniform beds. Today, the gardeners experiment with other compositions by using a range of cultivated and wild roses, including rose bushes, climbing or ground-cover roses, and roses winding around arches or shrubs.

Depending on the variety and the weather, the roses bloom between early summer and November. But the best time to admire them is in June, at the International Competition of New Roses. Since 1907, this event has awarded prizes to recently created roses—three for their beauty and one for its fragrance. During the competition, the flower candidates are displayed in the presenters' garden, which was specially designed for this purpose, and the park's gardeners give out valuable advice to enthusiasts.

"BAGATELLE: THESE LONG HOURS SPENT
IN A GARDEN ARE PERHAPS THE BEST THING
THAT WE WILL EVER HAVE HAD IN LIFE."
Henry de Montherlant

# THE NAME "PARC DE BAGATELLE"

♥ This park is steeped in so many stories that it can be difficult to untangle fact from fiction, even when it comes to its name, which has various connotations in French. It may refer to the park's low purchase price. Or perhaps to its modest size, compared to nearby properties. Or else to the amorous activities enjoyed by aristocrats at parties held in the garden during the ancien régime.

# Eighteenth-Century Manifesto

☞ Parc de Bagatelle encapsulates 18th-century garden fashions, which included nature in both a luxuriant and skillfully composed state; grottos; ruins that appear to be straight out of antiquity; and architecture inspired by an imagined East.

➥ When the park was built, English gardens prevailed in Europe. The aim was to recreate the spontaneity of nature in opposition to the symmetry of French gardens, which were considered too strict. But some found this imitation of nature too simplistic and decided to add complexity in the form of elements borrowed from China. Few architects in the 18th century had actually been to Asia, though, and the pagodas that cropped up in European parks have little in common with the originals.

➥ In Parc de Bagatelle, the Chinese pagoda and the Kiosque de L'Impératrice are primarily decorative buildings, but they provide advantageous views of the park.

# A Flower-Filled Walk

*While the rose is without doubt the star of the show at Parc de Bagatelle, many other plants flourish here throughout the year. The collections include 160 varieties of flowering bulbs that form colorful, ever-changing flowerbeds. Snowdrops kick things off in February, followed by crocus, narcissus, spring snowflake, tulips, and hyacinths into June.*

The Mediterranean garden is wilder in appearance than the rest of the park. It was created in 2000, after more than 300 trees were uprooted by a storm in 1999. It features species that are adapted to a dry, sunny climate, such as fig, heather, privet, and various aromatic plants. It is a precious source of inspiration for composing gardens that will be more adapted to future droughts. Chrysanthemums and clematis can be seen winding around trees or climbing walls, geraniums in the summer and fall, and, a little later in the year, asters, most of them from North America.

Water lilies thrive in the lake, where a splendid weeping willow is reflected. The largest plane tree in Paris, towering 148 feet (45 m) high, stands a little further away. Only the luckiest visitors are likely to spot a kingfisher near the coots, moorhens, and barnacle geese that frequent the lake. But no one can miss the peacocks—about 50 of them live in the park and enjoy the attention of visitors.

## JARDIN BOTANIQUE DE PARIS

Parc de Bagatelle, along with Parc Floral, the Paris arboretum, and the neighboring Auteuil greenhouses, forms part of the Paris Botanical Gardens and has received Jardin Remarquable status.

jardin
remarquable

# • PRACTICAL INFORMATION •

### OPENING HOURS
<u>Winter:</u> Open daily 9:30 a.m.–5 p.m.
<u>Spring:</u> Open daily 9:30 a.m.–6:30 p.m.
<u>Summer:</u> Open daily 9:30 a.m.–8 p.m.
<u>Fall:</u> Open daily 9:30 a.m.–6:30 p.m.

### TICKETS
Free entry <u>from October to March</u>
<u>April to September:</u> €2.50 | reduced price €1.50 | free for children under 7

### GETTING THERE
Pont de Neuilly (M. 1), Avenue Henri-Martin (RER C)

### AMENITIES AND ACTIVITIES
Playgrounds
Picnic tables
Exhibitions
Concerts (Octuor de France, Festival Chopin, Les Musicales, Lyrique au Vert, Les Solistes)

<u>April 1 to October 31:</u> guided tours are held at 3 p.m. every Sunday and on public holidays.

**paris.fr/lieux/parc-de-bagatelle-1808** (in French)

# 14

# PARC
# des Buttes-Chaumont
## Paris 19e

*A stroll through Buttes-Chaumont promises an escape into nature
with the vastness of the city in sight. Although this undulating park is entirely
man-made, many species of plants and animals thrive here.
With its central island surrounded by a lake, its hanging bridge,
and its rocky bluffs, this peaceful haven is full of surprises.*

Wandering around Parc des Buttes-Chaumont, visitors may be hard pressed to imagine that, less than two centuries ago, this charming park was the site of an inhospitable gypsum quarry. The area's 62 acres (25 ha) were transformed into a green space during the reign of Napoleon III, when Paris was being restructured by Baron Haussmann. The emperor wanted to give the working classes a place for leisure, but also to clean up the neighborhood—at the time, it was believed that harmful odors, referred to as "miasmas," emanated from insalubrious areas.

**ONE OF THE LOVELIEST GIFTS FROM THE SECOND EMPIRE TO PARIS IN A WORKING—CLASS NEIGHBORHOOD.**

Over a period of three years, the quarries were remodeled from top to bottom, and Parc des Buttes-Chaumont was inaugurated during the 1867 World's Fair. The work, overseen by engineer Jean-Charles Adolphe Alphand, took on gargantuan proportions: over 7,000,000 cubic feet (200,000 m³) of soil were necessary to make the park viable. Parc des Buttes-Chaumont is located on one of the highest points in the capital, giving it a panoramic view of the city that stretches all the way to the Sacré-Coeur Basilica. •

# A Man-Made Landscape

Buttes-Chaumont's unique charm is the result of a strange combination of artificial and natural elements. A fair number of boulders and wooden bridges in the park are actually made of a mix of concrete and cement. The lake is also artificial, as are the large grotto carved from the former quarries and its stalactites, which are nearly 30 feet (9 m) long. The park is inspired by English gardens, and the designers strove to create a variety of settings such as prairies, forests, and pavilions that can be contemplated like paintings. The park is overlooked by the Temple of Sibylle: a small architectural folie inspired by ancient Greco-Roman monuments.

## THE NAME "PARC DES BUTTES-CHAUMONT"

318   Paris.  Buttes Chaumont, Pont des suicides.

312   Paris.  Buttes Chaumont. le Parc.

The site is said to have been called Mont Chauve or Chauve-Mont ("bald mountain"), a term commonly used to refer to hills of gypsum or clay whose soil was sterile. Chaumont is thought to be a contraction of this name.

# Paradise for Parisians—and Plants

*Sprawling over nearly 62 acres (25 ha) in the 19th arrondissement, Buttes-Chaumont is one of the largest parks in the capital.*

In spring and summer, Parc des Buttes-Chaumont is the backdrop for an explosion of fragrance and color. The flowerbeds that line the paths are masterpieces of floral composition. Going off the beaten track, visitors will encounter many other plant varieties, such as comfrey, sweet violet, white campion, catalpa, and wild barley. Several remarkable trees have been planted in the park, including a

The constant presence of humans has not deterred the many birds that live here. Depending on the season, seagulls, ducks, moorhens, blackbirds, chickadees, jays, woodpeckers, and even parrakeets can be spotted here, as well as hedgehogs, red squirrels, and bats.

pagoda tree from Japan—which has been reflected in the lake since 1873—two ginkgo biloba, a Lebanese cedar, a giant sequoia, and Old World sycamores.

## A BIT OF HISTORY

Before it was transformed into a park, the Buttes-Chaumont area had a bad reputation. Until the 17th century, the Montfaucon gallows, where thousands of people were executed, stood nearby. The hills themselves were a kind of open-air dumping ground where horse carcasses were disposed of. The subsoil in the 19th arrondissement is rich in gypsum, and the Buttes-Chaumont deposit was mined from the late 18th century. At the time, the land was located in the commune of Belleville—a depressed area that did not become part of Paris until 1860. After that, the site was abandoned and became a place of ill repute where highway robbers would arrange to meet.

# • PRACTICAL INFORMATION •

## OPENING HOURS
<u>Fall and winter:</u> Open daily 7 a.m.–8 p.m.
<u>Spring:</u> Open daily 7 a.m.–9 p.m.
<u>Summer:</u> Open daily 7 a.m.–10 p.m.

## TICKETS
Free entry

## GETTING THERE
Buttes-Chaumont (M. 7 Bis), Laumière (M. 5)

## AMENITIES AND ACTIVITIES

Playgrounds
Sandboxes
Carousels
Dog park
Guignol puppet shows
Bandstand
Pony rides

Restaurant, cafeteria/
café, bars,
refreshment stand,
takeaway stand
Unrestricted access
to lawns

**paris.fr/lieux/parc-des-buttes-chaumont-1757**

*la seine*

# GARDENS
## AROUND PARIS

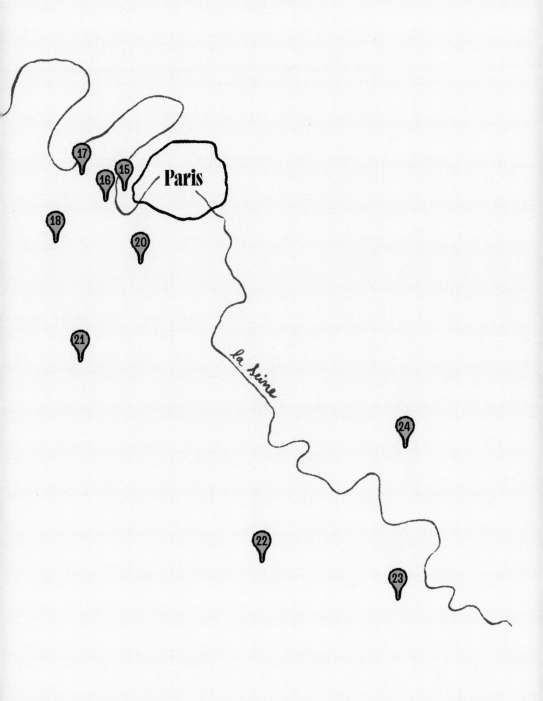

# 15

# JARDIN
# du Musée Albert-Kahn
## Boulogne-Billancourt

*Albert Kahn's incredible garden reflects the humanist philosophy
of its creator. In designing landscapes that evoke various regions of the world,
Kahn, a wealthy banker, sought to give shape to his deepest-held conviction:
that coexistence and universal peace are possible.*

A lbert Kahn was born in Alsace in 1860. As a child, he was deeply affected by the violence of the Franco-Prussian War, which resulted in the annexation of his native region by the German empire. At the age of 16, he moved to Paris, where he soon made his fortune. At just 38 years old, he was already director of his own bank. The businessman had plenty of money and ideas: he contributed to many philanthropic works and created a number of foundations to further his ideals of peace and harmony. In the late 19th century, he decided to settle in a wealthy residential area near the Seine—the aptly named Abondances neighborhood, which was then located in the town of Boulogne-sur-Seine. He was captivated by the beautiful environment and surrounding forest (the area is near Bois de Boulogne). In 1895, he undertook an incredible project to create a world-garden by gradually acquiring plots of land. Under his direction, landscape designer Achille Duchêne and other gardeners created landscapes representative of different continents and garden styles, including a French garden, an English garden, a Vosges forest, a Japanese village, and a wildflower meadow.

**THE MOST POWERFUL DEMONSTRATION OF CURIOSITY ABOUT THE WORLD AND OF LOVE FOR GARDENS.**

The large greenhouse is home to a wealth of exotic plants.

Ruined by the financial crisis in the late 1920s, Albert Kahn lost his garden in 1932. The Seine département gradually acquired it to make "a national conservatory for the art of gardening." The estate was opened to the public for the first time during the 1937 World's Fair.

Albert Kahn was a surprising individual—both pragmatic and dreamy, reserved and open. He often invited his friends to explore his garden, where different "scenes" constantly evolved through the gardeners' ongoing efforts. Notable visitors who were enthralled by the display include philosopher Henri Bergson, sculptor Auguste Rodin, and Indian writer Rabindranath Tagore. The garden is a meditative space, but it was also a place of leisure when Albert Kahn lived there; today, it remains full of life and hosts many events. The Musée Albert-Kahn is dedicated to the collections and projects of this extraordinary figure. •

# Around the World in a Garden

*The Albert Kahn garden includes several very different
landscape scenes separated by subtle transitional areas.
Walking through these features feels like embarking on a tour of the world.*

The Japanese village was created following Kahn's travels in the Japanese empire. In the late 19th century, Europe was overcome by a veritable obsession with Japan. Books of Japanese woodblock prints were in high demand, and the Japanese way of life provided inspiration for refined interiors and Eastern-style gardens. Kahn had a small village of pavilions built by a carpenter-mason who purposely traveled from Japan for the project. It once included a five-floor pagoda resembling a Buddhist temple. In this place steeped in spirituality, cherry trees blossom in the spring and beds of multicolored azaleas call to mind the silhouette of Mount Fuji.

In the 1990s, Fumiaki Takano, a Japanese landscape designer, created a contemporary Japanese garden in homage to Kahn that has two delightful red wooden bridges, a Himalaya cedar, and a weeping beech. Several porticos, koi carp, sculptures, stone paths, and Japanese lanterns leave visitors feeling as if they have been transported to Asia.

An entirely different atmosphere reigns in the French garden, which is reminiscent of André Le Nôtre's major works in the Tuileries and at Versailles. Here, nature has been tamed into large, uniform lawns, pruned bushes, and symmetrical flowerbeds to form a landscape resembling a 17th-century painting. Roses and fruit trees coexist in an orchard-rose garden. The French garden stretches to the foot of a majestic greenhouse where bonsai, palm trees, and lush vegetation thrive.

In the English garden, plants appear free to express themselves, but in reality the composition has been carefully thought out to offer visitors spectacular views. The large central lawn is surrounded by trees, rock gardens, and a small river traversed by a bridge made of imitation wood. There used to be a dairy and an aviary in this spot. In the spring, bulbs such as narcissus and crocus bloom here.

Finally, Kahn created three distinct forests from a wide variety of trees of different origins and colors. The Vosges forest is strikingly realistic: mossy boulders, resinous trees, and mountain plants cover the area, to which artificial contours were added to evoke the walking paths in Kahn's native region. The blue forest, which contains Atlas cedars and blue spruce, represents the meeting of America and Africa. The golden forest is home to spruce and birch, whose leaves turn yellow in the fall.

# THE MUSEUM

☞ The building that houses the Musée Albert-Kahn was renovated under the direction of Japanese architect Kengo Kuma. He applied the principle of *engawa*—unique to traditional Japanese architecture—which resonates with Kahn's ideals: the museum's interior spaces continuously communicate with the exterior spaces through the use of natural materials and many openings onto the garden.

The exhibition areas showcase the *Archives of the Planet*: a collection of tens of thousands of photographs made using the autochrome process and several films. Between 1909 and 1931, Kahn asked 12 photographers to travel to every continent and take photos that were representative of the diversity of cultures and landscapes in the early 20th century. These documents offer visitors rare insight into the last century.

For botany fans, the Vosges barn presents the many plant species that are found in the various gardens, as well as an overview of the site's history and of the ambitious undertaking to recreate it from period photographs.

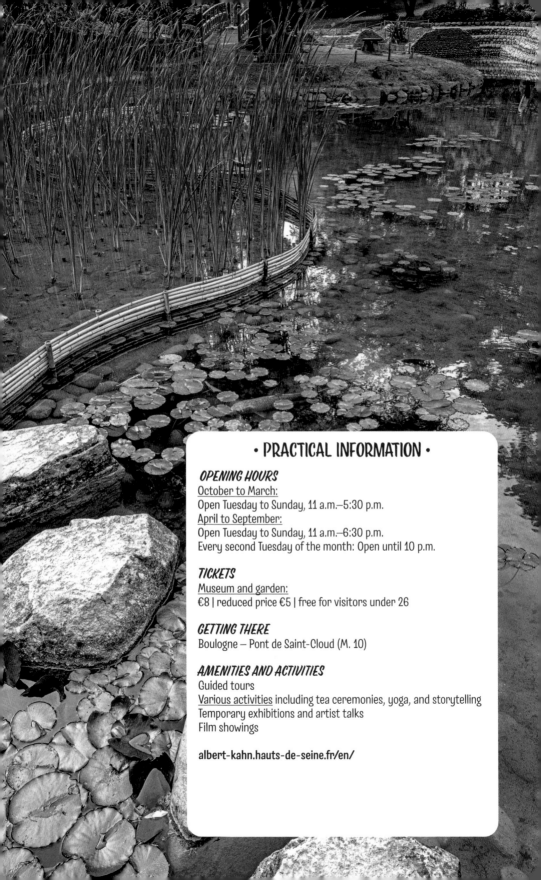

## • PRACTICAL INFORMATION •

### OPENING HOURS
October to March:
Open Tuesday to Sunday, 11 a.m.–5:30 p.m.
April to September:
Open Tuesday to Sunday, 11 a.m.–6:30 p.m.
Every second Tuesday of the month: Open until 10 p.m.

### TICKETS
Museum and garden:
€8 | reduced price €5 | free for visitors under 26

### GETTING THERE
Boulogne – Pont de Saint-Cloud (M. 10)

### AMENITIES AND ACTIVITIES
Guided tours
Various activities including tea ceremonies, yoga, and storytelling
Temporary exhibitions and artist talks
Film showings

albert-kahn.hauts-de-seine.fr/en/

# 16

# DOMAINE
# National de Saint-Cloud
## Saint-Cloud

*The vast Domaine de Saint-Cloud, which occupies 1,136 acres (460 ha),*
*offers a staggering view over the capital and its suburbs.*
*With water features, wooded areas, carpets of flowers, and a large terrace,*
*this is the perfect setting for long walks. In summer, thousands of people*
*gather here for the Rock en Seine music festival. Despite all these visitors,*
*the park seems haunted by an absence: not so very long ago,*
*a huge château stood here, surrounded by flowerbeds.*

Until it was definitively demolished in the late 19th century, the Château de Saint-Cloud was the scene of many major events in French history, including lavish parties, honeymoons, intrigues, and an assassination. Despite its prestigious past, almost no trace of the building remains. However, flowerbeds and cone-shaped yew trees mark its outline, giving visitors a chance to imagine the château for themselves.

The first occupant of Saint-Cloud was a certain Jérôme de Gondi, an agent of Catherine de Medici. He had an Italian-style garden built that has almost entirely disappeared, except for the Bassin du Grand Jet, which, as its name implies, produces a powerful stream of water. It was here, in 1589, during the Wars of Religion, that King Henry III was assassinated by a monk associated with the Holy League. In 1658, Louis XIV acquired the château. From then on, figures from the highest echelons of government were a constant presence within. The king gave the estate to his brother, the truculent Philippe d'Orléans, known as Monsieur, who had a French-style garden built with the help of the most sought-after landscape designer of the time, André Le Nôtre. Monsieur passed the estate on to his descendants, who resided there until Queen Marie Antoinette fell in love with the château in 1785; apparently she was captivated by its charm while riding through the area in her carriage.

**A PLACE WHERE THE PAST IS EVER-PRESENT.**

During the First French Empire, Saint-Cloud was the focus of much attention: Napoleon Bonaparte carried out his coup d'état of 18 Brumaire in the orangery on November 9, 1799. Several years later, he was proclaimed emperor in the Galerie d'Apollon, in a ceremony that would be symbolically reproduced by his nephew, Napoleon III, in 1852.

The Château de Saint-Cloud was an architectural masterpiece. There, in a residence removed from the hustle and bustle of Paris, sovereigns amassed treasures produced by the most well-known artists of their day. Napoleon I even wanted to transfer the *Mona Lisa* to Saint-Cloud, but fortunately his idea was rejected. Luckily, most of the masterpieces had already been transferred to museums when a terrible fire destroyed the château. In September 1870, during the Franco-Prussian war, Prussians invaded the building. Then, on October 13, 1870, an ill-fated shell shot by the French landed in the emperor's chambers and set off a spectacular blaze that left nothing but smoking remains in its wake. In 1891, the ruins were demolished by the government of the Third Republic, which cared little for vestiges of the ancien régime. •

The view from the Rond de la Balustrade.

# A WALK THROUGH THE CENTURIES

Today, the French garden that André Le Nôtre designed for Monsieur is clearly visible. It features characteristics typical of works carried out by the king's gardener: symmetry dominates the landscape, symbolizing human mastery of nature. The spaces are

↠ Several spaces have been remodeled or added to the park over the centuries. For example, Marie Antoinette, who loved flowers, created a flower garden intended to produce thousands of plants, including numerous roses. Today, many varieties are still grown there. The garden includes pretty little angled greenhouses and is often open to the public during certain events.

↠ The 19th century also left its mark on the park: the Trocadéro garden is a romantic space that reflects typical English design with its winding paths and lush vegetation. It is also home to several remarkable trees, including Lebanese cedar, maple, thuja, and a beautiful weeping beech arching over an artificial lake. More recently, a mosaic of flowers, whose pattern changes every year, was created on the Montretout hill overlooking the château terrace.

structured around two intersecting axes, one of which commands a view of more than 1¼ miles (2 km), and large openings alternate with more contained wooded areas. Le Nôtre also managed to make good use of the land's defects. Ambling along the terraces, up and down the flights of steps, and around the pools, visitors have the impression that they are walking through a setting that is at once varied and deeply harmonious.

Gérard Garouste, *Challenge to the Sun* (2013).
This enigmatic sculpture symbolizes the conflict between two opposing tendencies
that coexist within human beings: Apollonian and Dionysian, classicism and intuition.

## *JARDIN DU PIQUEUR*

♥ The Jardin du Piqueur is an
educational farm that includes a
vegetable garden, an orchard, and pastures
where animals graze—perfect for children!

# Saint-Cloud's Water Features

👉 The many pools and fountains that are scattered throughout the grounds are fed by a hydraulic network powered by the force of gravity alone. The large waterfall, built by Antoine Le Pautre and continued by Jules Hardouin-Mansart at the request of Monsieur, is certainly one of the most impressive water features in all the gardens in the Île-de-France region. When it is in operation, water gushes from stone mascarons, sea monsters, and frogs, and flows down over nine levels against a backdrop evoking rocky concretions; it is bordered by two bubbling artificial torrents. The waterfall, which has suffered somewhat over the years, is due to be entirely renovated by the French National Monuments Center.

# Musée Historique de Saint-Cloud

☞ The history museum at Saint-Cloud holds salvaged vestiges of the château, including a few dishes and seven statues from the facades. Visitors are invited to immerse themselves in the extraordinary history of the estate and its occupants through portraits, paintings, historical documents, and period photographs.

## THE PHANTOM OF THE CHÂTEAU

→ Using the Timescope—a virtual reality device—visitors can view the château's ghostly contours within the park itself.

## MUSÉE DE LA MANUFACTURE DE SÈVRES

♥ Since its creation in 1740, the Sèvres manufactory works has produced many porcelain wonders, including tableware, vases, sculpture, and furniture. Today, they can be viewed in the museum, which also regularly hosts fascinating temporary exhibitions.

## • PRACTICAL INFORMATION •

### OPENING HOURS
March, April, September, and October: 7:30 a.m.–8:50 p.m.
May to August: 7:30 a.m. to 9:50 p.m.
November to February: 7:30 a.m.–7:50 p.m.

### TICKETS
Free entry to the park
Musée de la Manufacture de Sèvres: €7 | reduced price €5 |
€1 supplement for temporary exhibitions

### GETTING THERE
Pont de Sèvres (M. 9), Boulogne – Pont de Saint-Cloud
(M. 10), Saint-Cloud (train lines L, U)

### AMENITIES AND ACTIVITIES
Guided tours
Bike paths
Temporary exhibitions
Restaurants: Le Brumaire, La Faisanderie,
    Le Fer à cheval, La Lanterne

**domaine-saint-cloud.fr/en**

# 17

# DOMAINE
# de la Malmaison
## Rueil-Malmaison

*La Malmaison will always be associated with Joséphine de Beauharnais
(1763–1814), who was, for a time, empress of the French.
Her passion for botany is less commonly known, though.
In 1799, she began reconfiguring the estate to turn it into a site
that was as unique as she was. Traces of the First Empire
and the lady of the house are still alive and well here today.*

Joséphine was right not to pay too much attention to the name La Malmaison ("the bad house"): she spent the best years of her life in this charming estate that she acquired in 1799 and where she drew her last breath. When she bought it, she was newly married to Napoleon Bonaparte, who became Napoleon I after a sensational coup d'état. There was a château on the property, but the couple found it outmoded and decided to carry out a complete renovation.

Charles Percier and Pierre Fontaine, two young architects, were responsible for the work. They transformed the château into a sort of modern Roman villa and laid the groundwork for Empire style. Greco-Roman references were everywhere, inside and out: sculptures, imitation marble columns, frescoes depicting mythological figures, chaises longues, and curule seats. In the 18th century, the interiors of royal residences had been rather exuberant, but after the French Revolution there was a tendency to associate this excessive ornamentation with decadent aristocracy. Tastes evolved toward a more pared-down style that was no less compatible with luxury. The archeological digs at Pompei were another inexhaustible source of inspiration for artists. Napoleon and Joséphine held many receptions at La Malmaison, and the château was one of the most important centers of power in the Empire: Napoleon had an impressive library there, where he wrote some of the articles that appeared in the French civil code, and that are still in force today.

**THE EMPIRE
OF ROSES.**

Joséphine focused most of her attention on the grounds, which she continued

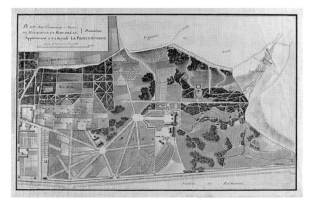

to enlarge, even after her marriage to Napoleon was annulled. Today, they occupy a relatively small space, but they once spanned nearly 1,800 acres (726 ha). The empress dreamed of having the most beautiful grounds in Europe. To offset the château's classicism, she had an English garden added, interspersed with openings and arbors, where nature was allowed to freely develop. A winding river runs through it, leading to an impressive greenhouse. This 4,300-square-foot (400-m²) glass cathedral, which can hold shrubs up to 16 feet (5 m) tall, is home to many exotic plants. Joséphine acclimated nearly 200 species to the Parisian climate—including some that have become fixtures in modern gardens, such as camellia, dahlia, and hibiscus. Explorers, scholars, and botanists from around the world sent them to her. The rest of the grounds feature many sculptures of Greco-Roman inspiration, as well as a Temple of Love, grottos, and a huge Lebanese cedar planted around 1800 by Napoleon and Joséphine. After the empress's death, the grounds no longer received the same level of care, and many of the plants withered away. In the early 20th century, after passing through the hands of several owners, the estate was acquired by the French state, which turned it into a museum devoted to the imperial couple; it also reintroduced some of the flowers that Joséphine particularly appreciated. •

# Rose or Joséphine?

Pierre-Paul Prud'hon,
*The Empress Joséphine* (1805).
Joséphine daydreams in the grounds
of La Malmaison, wearing the garb
of a Roman empress.

In her lifetime—and after her death—Joséphine was a subject of fascination. She was born Marie-Joseph-Rose de Tascher de la Pagerie in Martinique to a family of békés, the term used to designate descendants of the first colonists. Although she is sometimes described as a frivolous or adulterous woman, she was in reality a widow at just 32. Alexandre de Beauharnais, her first husband, had been executed during The Terror. It was only after she met Napoleon Bonaparte that people began calling her Joséphine, because Bonaparte did not like the name Rose. Crowned at the same time as her new husband, she was unable to bear him an heir on account of her age. The couple agreed to a divorce in 1809. Napoleon married Marie-Louise of Austria, with whom he had a son, Napoleon II; but the younger Napoleon only ruled two weeks before being deposed by Louis XVIII and died at the tender age of 21. Joséphine retained her imperial privileges—and the La Malmaison estate—until her death in 1814.

# THE ROSES OF LA MALMAISON

👉 Like Marie Antoinette before her, Joséphine was truly passionate about flowers—and roses in particular. At La Malmaison, she cultivated more than 200 different species, which she scattered along the paths, perhaps in remembrance of her former name.

➻ Roses were sent to her from around the world to enrich her collection; her gardeners also carried out grafts and experiments to create new varieties.

—

Above: The rose variety Souvenir de la Malmaison, created in 1843.

➻ At the empress's request, painter Pierre-Joseph Redouté made two volumes of watercolors and drawings: one representing rare plants present in the grounds, and the other exclusively featuring roses.

# THE MENAGERIE

LES CANGOUROUS A LA MALMAISON

♥ Joséphine's penchant for nature did not stop at plants: she also loved animals, especially the most exotic species. Shortly after acquiring the property, she had a sort of zoo built where she raised kangaroos, Australian black swans, ostriches, and even an orangutan and a zebra. The animals were given free rein to roam the grounds. Unfortunately, the results of the experiment were inconclusive, and most of the residents in this short-lived zoo were sent to the Jardin d'Acclimatation in 1805.

## Parc de Bois-Préau

☞ Visitors can extend their visit with a stroll through Parc de Bois-Préau, which was once part of La Malmaison's English-style grounds. The gently rolling park is home to several remarkable trees, including a Turkish hazel and a giant sequoia.

# • PRACTICAL INFORMATION •

## OPENING HOURS

**Park**
<u>October 1 to March 31:</u> Open 10 a.m.–6 p.m., closed Tuesday
<u>April 1 to September 30:</u> Open 10 a.m.–6:30 p.m., closed Tuesday

**Château**
<u>October 1 to March 31:</u> Open weekdays 10 a.m.–12:30 p.m. and 1:30 p.m.–5:15 p.m., closed Tuesday / Open weekends 10 a.m.–12:30 p.m. and 1:30 p.m.–5:45 p.m.
<u>April 1 to September 30:</u> Open weekdays 10 a.m.–12:30 p.m. and 1:30 p.m.–5:45 p.m., closed Tuesday / Open weekends 10 a.m.–12:30 p.m. and 1:30 p.m.–6:15 p.m.

## TICKETS

<u>Park:</u> €1.50
<u>Park and museum:</u> €6.50 | reduced price €5

## GETTING THERE

Rueil-Malmaison (RER A), then bus 258 to Le Chateau

## AMENITIES AND ACTIVITIES

Permanent and temporary exhibitions
Guided tours
Workshops for children

musees-nationaux-malmaison.fr/chateau-malmaison/en

# CHÂTEAU
## de Versailles
### Versailles

# 18

*Recognized as a symbol of France around the world, the Château de Versailles
will forever be associated with the Sun King. The château's luxuriant gardens
are André Le Nôtre's crowning achievement, where his talent was expressed
to the full. Here, nature is closely intertwined with culture, and the figure
of Apollo—Louis XIV's allegorical twin—is omnipresent.*

**AN UNMISSABLE
VISIT TO BE ENJOYED
IN STAGES.**

In 1682, the court of King Louis XIV relocated to Versailles. The king, who had been traumatized as a child by The Fronde—a revolt led by the nobility—wanted to keep an eye on the aristocracy by gathering them together somewhere near Paris. The original château was built on the orders of his father, Louis XIII. In 1660, Louis XIV began enlarging it with a series of additions. He also began transforming the gardens, which interested him greatly, perhaps even more so than the palace's architecture: he closely monitored the work and wanted to know about every last detail. The monumental work required draining the swamps located on the land and lasted for nearly 40 years. The gardens at Versailles are the masterwork of the king's gardener, André Le Nôtre, who created an enormous park where illusion and mise en scène reigned. The gardens as a whole are structured around the Grande Perspective: an open line of view that cuts through the landscape like an axis of symmetry. Around it are arranged groves that evoke rooms in a palace. The gardens had to be green all year long, so André Le Nôtre scattered easy-to-prune yew and box trees throughout. The large canal, which extends the view to the horizon, stretches for nearly a mile (1.6 km).

Over the centuries, the estate has undergone continual changes, including significant restoration campaigns in the 1990s. In 1979, the château and its grounds were added to UNESCO's list of World Heritage Sites. The gardeners who work here are driven by a passion for botanical history and strive to transmit Le Nôtre's vision as faithfully as possible by keeping skills and techniques from the past alive. •

## THE ORANGERY

Located below the château and out of the wind, the orangery in its present guise was built around 1683 by Jules Hardouin-Mansart. The parterres in the French-style gardens form harmonious winding patterns. In winter, the collection's orange, lemon, oleander, palm, and pomegranate trees—some of which are more than 200 years old—are kept inside, where they are protected from the cold by thick walls and double-glazed windows. In warmer weather, they are distributed among the parterres.

In the distance can be seen the Pièce d'Eau des Suisses: a huge 32-acre (13-ha) lake that was dug by an army of several thousand Swiss Guards. The blur of white among the trees is a sculpture by François Girardon, based on a work by the Italian sculptor Gian Lorenzo Bernini. The technically masterful work depicts Louis XIV taming the brute force of his rearing steed. Surprisingly, the king was not pleased with the sculpture, which was placed where he was unlikely to see it.

## BOSQUET DE LA SALLE DE BAL

In the days of Louis XIV, the gardens hosted many performances and other forms of entertainment, especially in the ballroom grove, also known as the rococo grove, which was designed to be an amphitheater, complete with grassy terraced seating. The arena originally included an islet surrounded by a canal. A waterfall made of marble and millstone—a porous and highly friable material—adorned with vases and seashells imported from the East and from Africa complete the fairy-tale setting.

# BOSQUET DE LA COLONNADE

The colonnade grove is a masterpiece of balance. It is surrounded by a peristyle of columns in different colored marbles. The sculpture in the center was created by François Girardon, who designed it to be admired from every angle. Proserpine is the daughter of Ceres, the goddess of agriculture and fertility. The statue depicts her abduction by Pluto, god of the underworld. When Ceres learns of her daughter's disappearance, she is inconsolable and stops attending to the earth. She strikes a deal with Pluto: her daughter can return to her side six months out of the year. Since then, nature has died every year when Proserpine leaves for the underworld and is reborn in spring, when she returns. The impression of lightness and fragility conveyed by Proserpine's arms is offset by the powerful massiveness of Pluto's legs, which seem to defy the slender body of Cyane, a nymph who tries to hold her friend back. Anger and violence are written on Pluto's face.

# BASSIN D'APOLLON

After the groves, the Grande Perspective is interrupted by the majestic Apollo's fountain, decorated with a gilded lead statue depicting the god's chariot. Every morning, Apollo (the Sun) bursts from the water to ride across the sky on his chariot. Here again, this representation of the triumphant god is an allusion to Louis XIV.

## BOSQUET DE L'ENCELADE

The Enceladus grove is probably the most impressive at Versailles. The fountain depicts the Titan Enceladus, who was buried under the boulders of Olympus by the gods. Here, he howls as he struggles among the rocks. When the fountain is in operation, a huge stream of water pours from his open mouth. Details are rendered with great precision: the hair on the back of his hand seem to bristle with fury. The grove is encircled by trellises that form architectural structures. These woven wooden elements are found everywhere in the gardens, where they demarcate the various spaces.

## BOSQUET DE LA REINE

The Queen's grove was once occupied by a labyrinth specially designed to educate the heir apparent. It contained fountains depicting Aesop's fables, which he was invited to reflect upon. Today, this space contains an English-style garden that was restored and is populated with a wide range of plants including roses, flowering shrubs, and perennials. There are also a number of Virginia tulip trees, which were Marie Antoinette's favorites.

## BIODIVERSITY AT VERSAILLES

A multitude of plants and animals live in the Sun King's former estate. The gardeners are committed to preserving this specific biodiversity by using cultivation methods that respect the environment. The celebrated gardener Alain Baraton is head of maintenance, conservation, and development in the gardens. The different spaces are home to many species of trees, including a pedunculate oak, near the Grand Trianon, that was alive when Louis XIV resided here.

Chestnut and linden are the most common trees at Versailles, but the gardens are also home to a pagoda tree that was planted in the 18th century, a Lebanese cedar, a catalpa, and a giant sequoia. An app developed by the château enables visitors to discover these witnesses to centuries past on a 14-stage tour of the garden.

Marie Antoinette was very fond of flowers. The gardeners pay tribute to her passion by taking special care of the estate's many flowerbeds featuring bulbs and perennials, as well as varieties cultivated near the Grand Trianon.

## Bassins des Saisons

At the intersection of the garden paths are four pools inhabited by divinities symbolizing the four seasons: Flora, for spring; Ceres, for summer; Bacchus, for fall; and Saturn, for winter (1677). The sculptures are made of lead, a highly malleable material.

# Sculptures

...................................

The gardens at the Château de Versailles are adorned with 824 statues. Originally, these were authentic masterpieces of French sculpture, but most of them have been transferred to museums and replaced by faithful copies in order to protect them from inclement weather. A few contemporary sculptures have been added in recent years.

Pierre Puget, *Milo of Croton* (1671–1682).
Milo was a former athlete who wanted to prove his strength by splitting a tree stump with his hand. But his fingers became trapped, and he was soon eaten by a lion. It is said that upon seeing the statue, Queen Maria Theresa of Austria cried out, "The poor man!"

Jean-Baptiste Tuby, Philibert Vigier, and Jean Rousselet,
*Laocoön and His Sons* (1684–1696).
This sculpture is based on a famous piece found in Rome in the 16th century.
During the Trojan War, Apollo sentenced the priest Laocoön and his two sons
to suffocation by sea monsters.

*Venus of Arles* (late first century BCE).
The Venus of Arles is a true Roman
sculpture. It was discovered in 1651
in several pieces in the Roman theater
in Arles. Sculptor François Girardon
restored it with little concern for
historical accuracy—not a priority
at the time—by adding arms, an apple,
and a mirror.

# Petit Trianon and Hameau de la Reine

In the far reaches of the park stands a set of buildings where Queen Marie Antoinette liked to withdraw, far from the royal court. The Petit Trianon is a parallelepiped pavilion crowned with a terrace—the architecture seems minimalist when compared to the ostentatious Château de Versailles. The surrounding gardens were designed in an English-Chinese style that was very popular in the late 18th century: nature appears to run free, but the landscape is, in reality, highly controlled. The nearby Temple de l'Amour (Temple of Love), a Greco-Roman-style building, gives the area a bucolic appearance.

Around the year 1777, Marie Antoinette asked Richard Mique to build a surprising architectural caprice—a sort of small village where she felt as though she were living a peasant's life. But everything was also highly contrived, including the reception cottages, ornamental pond, tower, dairies, fishing spot, boudoir, billiards room, and mill, whose wheel was merely decorative.

# · PRACTICAL INFORMATION ·

## OPENING HOURS

**Gardens**
High season: Open daily 8 a.m.–8:30 p.m.
Low season: Open daily 8 a.m.–6 p.m.

**Château**
High season: Open daily 9 a.m.–6:30 p.m., closed Monday
Low season: Open daily 9 a.m.–5:30 p.m., closed Monday

**Domaine de Trianon**
High season: Open daily noon–6:30 p.m., closed Monday
Low season: Open daily noon–5:30 p.m., closed Monday

## TICKETS

Free entry to the gardens, except during Grandes Eaux
and Jardins Musicaux events
Château: €18 | reduced price €14.50 | free for EU citizens under 26
Domaine de Trianon: €12 | reduced price €8 | free for EU citizens under 26

## GETTING THERE

Versailles Château – Rive Gauche (RER C), Versailles Rive Droite
(train line L), Versailles Chantiers (RER C, train lines N, U)

## AMENITIES AND ACTIVITIES

Guided tours
Restaurant: La Petite Venise
Performances
Tourist train
Row boats
Grandes Eaux Musicales
　(musical fountain shows)

Grandes Eaux Nocturnes
　(nighttime fountain shows,
　held in summer)
Jardins Musicaux
　(musical garden visits)

en.chateauversailles.fr

# DOMAINE de Villarceaux

## Chaussy

*Along with the châteaux of La Roche-Guyon, Ambleville, and Auvers-sur-Oise, the Domaine de Villarceaux is one of the gems of the Regional Natural Park of the Vexin Français. Located several miles from the border between the regions of Île-de-France and Normandy, it forms a patchwork of terraces, gardens, and buildings, with water as the central element.*

The Domaine de Villarceaux is uniquely located near the Epte, a tributary of the Seine, making it home to many springs that feed its large pools. Everything here is related to water, which shapes the landscape.

The lower château, whose foundations are literally steeped in water, was built around the late 11th or early 12th century. After being used to defend the French kingdom against Viking invasions, then against the English during the Hundred Years War, it became a vacation home that successive owners continually transformed according to their needs. In the 17th century, the Villarceaux manor, of which only a small part remains today, was home to Ninon de Lenclos: a renowned writer and courtesan of

**AN INTRICATE GARDEN BETWEEN SKY AND WATER.**

garden, turn right to walk between the Vinette pond and the pool with eight water spouts. The owners used to raise fish in several of the ornamental ponds on the grounds. Fish were highly appreciated by aristocrats, especially on days of abstinence when consuming meat was forbidden: this activity was, therefore, an important source of income for the château.

🐟 Further along is a garden inspired by Renaissance Italy. Topiaries—bushes pruned into original shapes—break up the park's dominant horizontal lines. The terrace opens onto the Bassin du Miroir, whose surface reflects the upper château, then onto the large lake. •

legendary beauty. The Saint-Nicolas tower, which resembles a small keep, is one of the last vestiges of the medieval period.

☸ This tower adjoins the Jardin des Simples: a medieval-inspired garden. Here, medicinal and aromatic plants are grown in square beds, as was the custom in the Middle Ages. After crossing the

# An Ambitious Restoration Project

In the 19th century, several of the gardens that can be visited at Villarceaux today were covered over with soil.

A large-scale restoration project brought this incredible landscape out into the light. Under the supervision of landscape designers Alain Cousseran and Allain Provost, and the head architect for France's historic monuments, Pierre-André Lablaude, the gardens and buildings were restored to their original splendor. The estate's current appearance reflects the many changes that have taken place there over time.

The Domaine de Villarceaux was awarded Jardin Remarquable status in 2005 and the Espace Vert Écologique label in 2012. Indeed, the park is truly a model of environmentally responsible management. The gardeners avoid using any chemical products that could be harmful to the environment, use compost produced by vermicomposting—made by worms—and remove unwanted plants by hand. The buildings are heated with geothermal energy, which draws from heat naturally present underground. Thanks to these respectful techniques, the grounds attract all kinds of animals: birds including ducks, swans, herons, and cormorants appreciate the ponds full of fish, and the wooded areas are home to squirrels, foxes, deer, and even bats.

# GARDEN ON THE WATER

During a walk through the park, the visitor's eye is constantly drawn toward a magnificent parterre embellished with box trees and canals that seems to hover above the water, between the large lake and the pool with eight water spouts. Reconstructed in the 1980s based on 17th-century plans, it is thought to have been created during the Renaissance as an analogy for human life. Life may seem like a maze sometimes, but after overcoming its obstacles, humans attain eternal life, represented here by a round pool.

♥ Yes, the Domaine de Villarceaux is home to the legendary fountain of youth—or at least one of the many fountains that claim the title.

☞ It is said that Ninon de Lenclos came here every day to freshen up, which apparently explains how her incredible beauty lasted into old age.

# The Upper Château

➻ In the mid-18th century, Charles Jean Baptiste du Tillet de La Bussière, marquis of Villarceaux, decided to build a residence more in line with contemporary fashions than the lower château. He was, however, receptive to the latter's picturesque appeal, so he preserved a part of it, which he made into a sort of medieval-inspired setting.

➻ The upper château, so named for its position dominating the grounds, is showcased by a magnificent *vertugadin*, or sloping lawn—a sculpture made from the landscape itself. The French term is derived from the structure used by women to support their skirts (farthingale in English). This one is composed of a series of lawns that keep pace with the slope of the land. They are decorated with 14 sculptures from the Palazzo Altieri in Rome and the Villa d'Este on Lake Como. From the summit, visitors have a view of the Vexin plateau, which alone is worth the climb.

➻ Certain rooms in the château are also open to visitors and present a delightful collection of late rococo furnishings. The rococo style, inspired by nature's exuberance, was incredibly popular during the first half of the 18th century. Around 1750, when the château was being built, this form of decorative expression took on a more subdued look with a return to more symmetrical forms. Nearby, an orangery with two greenhouses allowed the château owners to grow exotic fruit.

## • PRACTICAL INFORMATION •

### OPENING HOURS
<u>Early April to late October:</u>
Open 2 p.m.–6 p.m., closed Monday

### TICKETS
Free entry

### GETTING THERE
Cergy Saint-Christophe (RER A),
then bus 95-04 to Gare Routière,
followed by bus 95-43 to Villarceaux

### AMENITIES AND ACTIVITIES
Guided tours
<u>Guesthouse:</u> La Bergerie de Villarceaux

**villarceaux.iledefrance.fr** (in French)

# DOMAINE
# Départemental
# de la Vallée-aux-Loups
## Châtenay-Malabry

*Situated several miles from Paris, Vallée-aux-Loups—a huge 150-acre (61-ha) estate—was appreciated by several artists and landscape designers for its idyllic climate and exceptionally fertile soil. Now managed by the Hauts-de-Seine département, it comprises four spaces connected by the Aulnay stream: a wooded park, the Île Verte, the arboretum, and the residence of the famous writer François-René de Chateaubriand (1768–1848).*

Vallée-aux-Loups once served as a reservoir to feed the large water features at the Château de Sceaux, which was owned by French statesman Jean-Baptiste Colbert in the 17th century; the land, located at the bottom of a valley, contains many sources of water. However, it is probably Chateaubriand who made the area famous when he found refuge here from 1807 to 1817. After drawing the ire of Napoleon Bonaparte by comparing the French emperor to Nero, he decided to retire to this leafy setting away from Paris. To Chateaubriand, Vallée-aux-Loups was more than just a residence: all around his house, the writer—a great botany enthusiast—created a landscape that echoed his deepest aspirations.

## HORTICULTURAL CURIOSITIES AND THE SPIRIT OF CHATEAUBRIAND.

The Croux family, who built a plant nursery at Vallée-aux-Loups in 1856, had a similar passion for plants. For several generations, the family cultivated a variety of flowers, shrubs, and trees on nearly 250 acres (100 ha). The huge arboretum was initially designed as a living catalog that the Croux proudly presented to their clients. Today, it is home to many remarkable tree species, making it an unmissable visit for tree lovers.

In addition to several wooded areas, the Domaine de la Vallée-aux-Loups also includes the Île Verte, formerly a private property, where an ivy-covered house sits within a lush garden. In the 19th century, Jules Barbier—a renowned librettist—lived in this otherworldly place. Nearly a century later, the painter Jean Fautrier settled

at the Île Verte after a harrowing experience here during World War II. While a member of the Resistance, he found refuge in Chateaubriand's former home, which had been converted into a psychiatric hospital in the 1910s; for many long days, he heard the shootings carried out by the Gestapo in the woods around the house.

Vallée-aux-Loups is a site that is both steeped in history and ideal for finding peace. To preserve this microcosm where plants thrive, the gardeners use growing methods that are respectful of the environment. This means the various spaces are managed in different ways: some are meticulously maintained, while others are left to freely develop. Pests in the flowerbeds are removed using natural predators, which eliminates the need for chemical products. •

### "THE PROMISED LAND OF PARISIAN HORTICULTURE."
Édouard André

The Chateaubriand rose: a variety created by rose breeder Michel Adam in tribute to the writer.

# Chateaubriand and His Trees

*Chateaubriand traveled widely. During the French Revolution, he sought refuge in America, where he deepened his knowledge of botany. Several years later, he traveled through the Middle East, including Turkey. In fact, it was his contact with the Ottoman Empire that prompted him to turn a critical eye on the French Empire.*

In 1807, the writer alerted his contemporaries to the potential dangers of this regime in an article that earned him the suspicion of Napoleon I. To escape, he went into voluntary exile at Vallée-aux-Loups. Chateaubriand permanently modified the landscape by having a hill leveled and replaced by a vast lawn. He was soon spending most of his time in his garden, where he worked in the Velleda tower and planted thousands of flowers and trees. He considered the latter as beings in their own right, which served both as reminders of the countries he had traveled through and allusions to his dreams for the future. Despite a devastating storm in 1999, many have survived to the present day, including Greek cypresses, a Lebanese cedar, an Indian horse chestnut, an Algerian blue cedar, and a Virginia tulip tree.

While strolling through the park, visitors might catch a glimpse of an impressive catalpa from Louisiana that was destroyed by lightning and took root again. A true collector, Chateaubriand called on those he knew to acquire new rare species. The former empress Joséphine gifted him a magnolia with purple flowers from her Domaine de la Malmaison. François-René and Céleste de Chateaubriand lived in a house with a rather simple facade, preceded by a small Roman-style porch supported by two caryatids that give it a touch of originality. The interiors—now open to the public—are furnished in a style typical of the 19th century: many events are held there to keep the writer's memory alive. Chateaubriand was forced to leave the house for financial reasons in 1817, at a time when most of the trees he

had planted had not yet reached maturity. Today, visitors can enjoy the park just as he imagined it.

After belonging to the Montmorency and La Rochefoucauld families, the estate was sold in the early 20th century to two psychiatrists who set up a hospital there. Chateaubriand never forgot this meditative place that delighted his mind and senses. In *Memoirs from Beyond the Grave*, he wrote, "Of all the possessions I have lost, Vallée-aux-Loups is the only one I regret."

## THE WOODED PARK

♥ Visitors can extend their tour by taking a stroll
through the wooded park: a small forest where several
species of birds have made their home, including chickadees,
woodpeckers and—more difficult to observe—tawny owls,
sparrow hawks, and kestrels.

The exceptional bonsai collection at Vallée-aux-Loups.

# The Arboretum

This tree collection was developed by the Croux family nursery owners to impress their clients, who could choose from the species presented in landscape scenes arranged around a lake.

plants, whose descendants now populate the estate's themed gardens including a flower garden, a hydrangea garden, and a Styracaceae garden. They also used cross-breeding to create new

↦ The uncontested king of the arboretum is a magnificent weeping blue cedar whose large branches stretch out over the water. It is the first specimen of this species, which is the result of a mutation of the blue Atlas cedar that occurred right here. A veritable cathedral of greenery, the tree occupies about 7,500 square feet (700 m²). The gardeners take very good care of it: every seven years or so, they remove dead wood that has accumulated on its boughs so that it can grow freely.

↦ At the water's edge, visitors can observe a pond cypress with strange roots called pneumatophores that emerge from the ground: these asphyxiated roots travel through soil to reach the open air, where they can absorb oxygen.

↦ Many of the trees in the arboretum are over 100 years old and include oak, alder, bald cypress, Caucasian walnut, sequoia, and chestnut. The Croux family cultivated many other local and exotic

varieties, such as the famous "blue bird" rhododendron.

↦ The arboretum comprises several uncultivated spaces, including a meadow that is regularly hand-mowed. The park prohibits all motorized vehicles that might possibly damage tree roots. The lawns are maintained using the most natural mowers possible—Ouessant sheep.

"I AM ATTACHED TO MY TREES; I HAVE ADDRESSED
ELEGIES, SONNETS, AND ODES TO THEM. THERE IS NOT ONE
OF THEM THAT I HAVE NOT TENDED WITH MY OWN HANDS,
THAT I HAVE NOT RESCUED FROM ROOT–BEETLES, FROM
CATERPILLARS STUCK TO ITS LEAVES. I KNOW THEM ALL
BY NAME, AS IF THEY WERE MY CHILDREN:
THEY ARE MY FAMILY, I HAVE NO OTHER,
AND I HOPE TO DIE AMONG THEM."

François-René de Chateaubriand

## A MUSEUM OF CONVOLVULACEAE

☞ Do you rip out bindweed from your garden? This plant is often considered a weed, and for good reason: a strong climber, it tends to encroach somewhat on the territory of neighboring plants. But it is entirely possible to control bindweed without completely uprooting it, by just giving it enough space and keeping it away from plants that it deprives of light.

☞ Bindweed is a member of the large family of Convolvulaceae, characterized by five fused petals that bloom for a day or less before closing again. This family also includes volubilis, morning glory, and sweet potato. All of these species offer an incredible diversity of forms and colors.

☞ The national collection of Convolvulaceae at Vallée-aux-Loups is home to a multitude of varieties, including some that are endangered due to their bad reputation.

Île Verte: a peaceful, leafy haven.

## Jardin de L'Aigle Blanc

The Château d'Aulnay once stood where the Jardin de L'Aigle Blanc (garden of the white eagle) now lies. This former residence of Count Alexandre Colonna Walewski—the unacknowledged son of Napoleon I—is surrounded by wrought-iron railings. Recently restored, the area forms a pleasant enclave between the arboretum, the Île Verte, and the wooded park, offering splendid views over the estate's various spaces. Visitors may also stop there to picnic on its lawns or in its clearings, recline on the wooden deckchairs, or enjoy the playground.

## • PRACTICAL INFORMATION •

### OPENING HOURS
Each section of the estate has its own opening hours.
Visit the website (see below) for more information.

### TICKETS
Free entry to the park
Maison de Chateaubriand: €4 | reduced price €3 |
free for EU citizens under 26
€1 supplement during temporary exhibitions

### GETTING THERE
Robinson (RER B), then bus 179 to Vallée-aux-Loups

### AMENITIES AND ACTIVITIES
Exhibitions
Guided tours
Conferences
Tea room: Les Thés Brillants

**vallee-aux-loups.hauts-de-seine.fr/** (in French)

# 21

# CHÂTEAU
# de Saint-Jean-de-Beauregard
## Saint-Jean-de-Beauregard

*Saint-Jean-de-Beauregard, in the Essonne département,*
*is the perfect place to rediscover forgotten plants and growing methods.*
*In addition to a 5-acre (2-ha) vegetable garden, which looks pretty much*
*as it did in the 17th century, visitors will find a magnificent château,*
*sprawling grounds, and a period dovecote. The estate is a valuable*
*source of inspiration and information for home gardeners.*

Saint-Jean-de-Beauregard is a world unto itself. Over the years, its various occupants saw to it that they were surrounded with everything they needed to live well here, including French-style grounds, a dovecote, an orangery, stables, and a chapel. The vegetable garden and orchard supplied them with a variety of fruits and vegetables all year round. The current owners have revived this spirit by restoring the vegetable garden and turning it into a full-fledged conservatory of rare and heritage species. They have also made a point of upholding the artistry and techniques of bygone times. The estate's authentic character has been preserved for centuries through careful conservation of buildings and the original layout; as a result, it was classified a historic monument in 1993 and awarded Jardin Remarquable status in 2005. The château's architecture is typical of the 17th century: the building is crowned with a splendid sloping roof and large chimneys that emphasize its verticality. The residence is now inhabited by the Curel family, who open its rooms decorated with antique furniture to visitors during guided tours. The grounds have been open to the public since 1984.

**A UNIQUE HISTORIC VEGETABLE GARDEN.**

Twice a year, in spring and fall, Saint-Jean-de-Beauregard opens its doors for the Fête des Plantes. Nursery owners, farmers, horticulturalists, and specialists gather at the estate for this plant festival, where they share their creations and expertise.

These events are a must for nature lovers: heritage vegetables and new varieties of flowers are presented, and visitors can participate in hands-on classes and attend conferences about different gardening techniques. •

# The Vegetable Garden

*The walled vegetable garden has conserved the same general layout since the 17th century. Featuring the symmetrical arrangement typical of French-style gardens that was fashionable at the time, it is composed of four large square areas, each with a round, central pool used for watering. Each square is divided into four sub-plots.*

This perfect geometry serves more than just an aesthetic purpose—it enables crops to be rotated over a four-year period, as was customary in the past.

❧ The flowered borders that surround each plot grace the vegetable garden with a thousand colors, but they also provide protection for the produce from disease and insects without resorting to chemical products. The borders form monochrome compositions of warm or cool colors. Depending on the time of the year, Saint-Jean-de-Beauregard boasts hellebore, peony, iris, clematis, dahlia, and aster.

❧ An extremely diverse array of plant varieties is cultivated here. Besides the familiar carrots, turnips, lettuces, and tomatoes, the vegetable garden contains a collection of more unusual species, such as the common evening primrose, also known as "gardener's ham"—its root resembles a rosy white carrot and takes on a surprising taste of smoked ham when cooked—square peas, and various kinds of heirloom gourds.

❧ At the far end of the vegetable garden, grapevines grow in charming 19th-century greenhouses. The fruit itself is protected using a centuries-old, artisanal process known as the Thomery method, which shields it from extreme temperatures for several months. The greenhouses are located next to an orchard where plum, apple, cherry, and quince trees grow, as well as several types of heritage roses. The estate's owners have the ingredients for a variety of dishes and desserts at their fingertips.

*"COLOR, FLOWERING, ELEVATION—IT'S ALL HERE IN MY HEAD. IT'S BEEN A PASTIME OF MINE SINCE I WAS A CHILD."*
Muriel de Curel

## The Park

In keeping with 17th-century tradition, the estate also has an extensive park that was originally intended to host hunting parties and today offers visitors a welcome coolness in summer. This space, too, is rigorously composed according to the principles of French-style gardens, with groves and clearings that are clearly demarcated by straight paths lined with arbors. Here, again, the lawns are maintained using an age-old and environmentally-friendly method: sheep!

## THE DOVECOTE

↳ The dovecote at Saint-Jean-de-Beauregard is one of the oldest and largest of its kind in the Île-de-France region. It has 4,500 putlog holes: small niches carved in the walls to accommodate pigeons. Until the French Revolution, only members of the nobility were allowed to own dovecotes. At the time, pigeons were a precious resource because they provided eggs and meat, as well as guano: a fertilizer obtained from bird droppings that was used to enrich vegetable gardens.

# • PRACTICAL INFORMATION •

### OPENING HOURS
March 15 to November 15:
Open Sundays and public holidays 2 p.m.–6 p.m.

### TICKETS
Vegetable garden, grounds, and dovecote: €8 |
reduced price €6 | free for children under 6
Guided tour of the château and dovecote: €2 supplement

### GETTING THERE
Orsay Ville (RER B), then bus 5 to Lycée Essouriau

### AMENITIES AND ACTIVITIES
Free parking
Guided tours
Activity booklets and games
    for children
Easter egg hunt

Fête des Plantes
    in spring and fall
Fête de la Création et des
    Métiers d'Art in spring

**chateaudesaintjeandebeauregard.com** (in French)

# 22

# DOMAINE
## de Courances
### Courances

*Water structures everything at Courances, and, more precisely, running water—the* eau courante *alluded to in its name. The murmur of a fountain or the lapping of a stream is audible from just about anywhere on the property. Although the layout of the grounds exhibits the classicism of gardens à la française, a balanced blend of different styles and the ever-present influence of nature create a unique atmosphere at this estate located between Paris and Fontainebleau.*

A large pathway cuts through the grounds at Courances, leading to a majestic Louis XIII-style château. The horseshoe-shaped staircase rising to the château's entrance is similar in many ways to the one at the Château de Fontainebleau. For five generations, Courances has been home to the de Ganay family, who continue to maintain and transform the estate.

Long attributed to André Le Nôtre, the 185-acre (75-ha) park is, in reality, a delicate patchwork of overlapping elements added by successive owners. The earliest works still visible today were carried out by Cosme

Clausse in the 16th century. This French statesman installed an extraordinary autonomous hydraulic network that still supplies the many fountains and pools throughout the grounds. He also created a large canal that is thought to have inspired the one at Fontainebleau.

**"THE WOODS OF CÉLY, MEADOWS OF FLEURY, AND WATER OF COURANCES ARE ALL THREE MARVELS IN FRANCE."**
*Proverb recited in the court of Louis XIII*

Veuë du Chasteau de Courance en Gastinois.

Israel Henriet ex. cum privil. Regis

⧗ Claude Gallard, another member of the nobility, acquired Courances next and gave the grounds a more classical appearance. Between 1622 and 1630, he had the château built. In the 18th century, a large reflecting pool was added behind it. Preceded by two parterres of intricate box tree arabesques, this magnificent rectangular water feature covering nearly 2 acres (1 ha) reflects the château's facade and accompanies the eye as it travels

along a perspective that stretches into the distance.

⧗ In the late 19th century, the château was purchased by Baron Samuel de Haber, who had it restored in 17th-century style by architect Hippolyte Destailleur. The building had been left in such a state of neglect that a tree had begun to grow through the roof. The estate then passed to Baron de Haber's granddaughter, Marquise Berthe de Ganay, and her husband. They commissioned landscape designers Henri Duchêne and his son Achille—who also worked on the Albert Kahn garden—to renovate the grounds at Courances, where the two men implemented their ideal of a renewed classicism.

⧗ After being occupied by the Germans—who did a great deal of damage—during World War II, the estate was modernized by Jean-Louis de Ganay, who simplified the layout. He built large paths covered in carpets of greenery and lined with hedges, and gave nature the necessary space to grow. The château's current occupants are committed to preserving the many layers of history reflected in these extraordinary grounds while bringing them into the present day. The trees are no longer pruned in strict parallelepiped shapes, and the pools are cleaned by carp out of concern for the environment. The estate is now open to the public, and many guided tours and activities are held here. •

## A Cup of Tea?

After a visit to the Anglo-Japanese garden, the nearby La Foulerie is the perfect place to take a break. In the 17th century, it was the site of a hemp mill, where hemp was processed, or "*foulé*" in French, hence the building's name. Today, it is a delightful tea room that serves delicious pastries.

# THE ANGLO–JAPANESE GARDEN

Berthe de Ganay designed the Anglo-Japanese garden at Courances in the 1930s. Japanese-inspired gardens were very fashionable in the early 20th century, as evidenced by numerous turn-of-the-century examples including Claude Monet's garden at Giverny, the Parc Oriental at Maulévrier, and the Albert Kahn garden. The French discovered Japanese art at the 1867 World's Fair; following this event, many people were gripped by *japonisme*—a fascination with Japanese culture that had a lasting influence on every artistic field, including painting and printmaking, as well as interior and garden design, and fashion. Here, Berthe de Ganay implemented techniques such as pruning trees to resemble clouds, but the references to Japan remain exceedingly subtle. There are no Buddhist sculptures, pagodas, or lanterns, but rather a wide variety of gauzy or dense plants that form a nuanced palette, from bright red Japanese maple in fall to purple beech, Persian ironwood, bamboo, geranium, rose, and more. A small wooden bridge completes the scene.

Twenty-two gardeners once worked at Courances; today, four people are responsible for maintaining the water features, caring for the plants, and pruning the intricate box tree arabesques. Here, untamed nature is everywhere, especially in the woodland scenes, which are home to ferns and carpets of perennials, as well as a few imitation ruins scattered about—in typical 19th-century fashion—by architect Hippolyte Destailleur. Courances is famous for the plane trees that line its large pathway and seem to bow before visitors. A majestic 200-year-old plane tree stands at the edge of the Grande Perspective, behind the château, just before the Rond de Moigny. The estate also has a vegetable garden and agricultural land where many kinds of vegetables and plants are grown without the use of pesticides, and where agroforestry techniques (planting trees and hedges among crops) are practiced.

## A Remarkable Garden

. . . . . . . . . . . . . . . . . . . . . . . . . . . . . .

jardin remarquable

In 2005, the French Ministry of Culture granted the park at Courances Jardin Remarquable status. The château has been classified as a historic monument since 1983.

In 2016, the movie *C'est La Vie!* (*Le Sens de la fête* in French), directed by Olivier Nakache and Éric Toledano, was filmed at Courances.

# • PRACTICAL INFORMATION •

### OPENING HOURS
<u>Late March to early November:</u> Open weekends and public holidays 2 p.m.–6 p.m.

### TICKETS
<u>Grounds:</u> €9 | reduced price €7 | free for children under 7
<u>Guided tour of the château</u> (weekends and public holidays, in April, June, and September): €12 | reduced price €10 | free for children under 7

### GETTING THERE
Corbeil Essonnes (RER D), then bus 4346 to Château

### AMENITIES AND ACTIVITIES
Guided tours
Workshops
Tea room: La Foulerie
Restaurant
Vivier du Bien-Être (wellness space)

en.domainedecourances.com

# 23

# CHÂTEAU
# de Fontainebleau
## Fontainebleau

*It's no coincidence that every ruler since Francis I
has made this vast 320-acre (130-ha) estate their vacation home.
Napoleon I called it "the true home of kings, the house of ages."
Visitors to the Château de Fontainebleau and its large gardens,
which have been expanded over the centuries, walk in the footsteps
of the most illustrious figures in French history.*

## A FANTASTIC KALEIDOSCOPIC GARDEN.

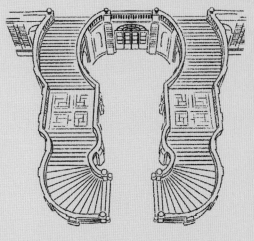

The château is surrounded by gardens of different styles that were created by successive occupants of the property, and reveal how tastes and fashions have evolved over the last three centuries. The French-style garden dominates several areas of the estate, especially those with ceremonial purposes or devoted to pageantry. A strict symmetry imbues the parterre and the pruned shrubs with a grandeur perfectly suited to the château's architecture. The main courtyard is structured around four uniform lawns and leads to a magnificent horseshoe-shaped staircase whose original form has made it the symbol of the château.

Behind the château, the large parterre, designed by André Le Nôtre—gardener to Louis XIV, who would, several years later, oversee construction of the gardens at the Château de Versailles—is also composed of four lawns, each with a large rectangular pool in the center. The garden is huge and rather windy in fall and winter. Previously, it was embellished with intricate box tree arabesques that, when seen from above, formed a tapestry of greenery.

☛ At the far end of the garden is a round pool decorated with an allegory of the Tiber River. A vast parterre overlooks the large canal, which was built at the request of Henry IV. The sheer size of this ornamental lake was unprecedented when it was built; it stretches for nearly 1.2 miles (2 km), creating a perspective that stretches as far as the eye can see.

☛ The garden of Diana owes its name to a sculpture representing Diana, the goddess of wild animals and the hunt. It is also known as the queen's garden, because it neighbors the apartments where various female monarchs resided over the centuries. In this more secret location, tucked away, nature is allowed to develop more freely than in the French-style gardens. Up to the reign of Louis-Philippe, it was bounded by an orangery. It took on its current appearance in the early 19th century. Visitors can rest on small stone benches and admire rare trees, such as a catalpa and a Virginia tulip tree. The English garden, also designed in the 19th century, is a pleasant area with a natural appearance, traversed by small paths and an artificial stream.

☛ The Étang aux Carpes (carp lake) is one of Fontainebleau's most picturesque spots. Francis I had it made from what was previously a marsh. A small decorative pavilion erected during the reign of Louis XIV seems to float above the waters. •

## DIANA, THE HUNTRESS OF FONTAINEBLEAU

This graceful bronze statue visible in the garden of Diana is a copy of a Greco-Roman sculpture.

Pope Paul IV gifted the marble original to Henry II in 1556. The king could not help but be captivated by this masterpiece that was brought to life by the twirling movement of the goddess and her little leaping deer—it probably reminded him of his mistress, Diane de Poitiers.

☛ The version in the garden at Fontainebleau was cast in 1684. It stands on a fountain surrounded by four dogs and four stag-head trophies that evoke the pleasures of hunting—an activity that has been popular with kings throughout history.

# A Château Steeped in History

The *Château de Fontainebleau was originally a hunting lodge in the heart of the forest. To this day, a keep located in the oval courtyard stands as a reminder of its medieval past. The estate acquired its prestigious reputation in the early 16th century during the reign of Francis I, who decided to build a sumptuous Italianate palace there. He made it a center of influence for the French Renaissance, attracting architects and artists from all backgrounds.*

The château was completed by the king's son, Henry II, who ordered the construction of the first version of the sumptuous horseshoe-shaped staircase—one of Fontainebleau's most iconic elements—in the main courtyard, as well as a ballroom with a magnificent gold and silver coffered ceiling. A second version of the staircase

was built under Louis XIII. In the early days of Louis XIV's reign, Fontainebleau was the stage for a kind of dress rehearsal for the court ceremonies celebrating the king's glory that he later established at Versailles. The court gathered here around the young monarch. It was during this period that André Le Nôtre entirely redesigned the gardens and created the large parterre. Under Louis XV, architect Ange-Jacques Gabriel imprinted the residence with a classical charm, still very influenced by Renaissance exuberance and Italian mannerism. Marie Antoinette very much appreciated Fontainebleau, where she had a Turkish boudoir installed—a place she could retire to, away from court intrigues. In the late 18th century, *turqueries*—decorative elements vaguely inspired by the East—were extremely popular with members of the king's entourage. This room, with windows overlooking the garden of Diana, was later redecorated by Empress Joséphine. Despite the destruction of much of its furniture during the French Revolution, the Château de Fontainebleau has always been relatively protected from the vagaries of French history and bears traces of every period it has witnessed. It was one of Napoleon I's favorite residences, and the château is now home to a museum devoted to the emperor; it features objects and surprising reconstructions, such as the interior of the tent in which he slept during his military campaigns. Napoleon III and the empress were the last rulers to have set up quarters in the château, where they held unforgettable parties.

## THE MYSTERIES OF FRANCIS I

Before or after a stroll in the garden, visitors should take time to walk through the château's Grande Galerie; Francis I brought in Italian masters like Rosso Fiorentino and Francesco Primaticcio to embellish it with frescoes and extremely complex motifs. Certain scenes may be difficult to understand—which was precisely the king's intention. He was the only person who knew what they meant and used that fact to impress his guests with his knowledge. As his sister, Marguerite de Navarre, wrote, "Seeing your works without you is a lifeless body, and looking at your buildings without hearing your thoughts about them is like reading Hebrew." At the king's behest, Primaticcio also created the Grotte des Pins (pine grotto) in the château grounds. Three atlantes made from boulders blend into the scenery of this strange artificial grotto, which opens onto a garden populated by maritime pines. An exotic species hitherto unknown in the region, these trees must have surprised visitors.

> *"I WOULD LIKE FOR ALL FRENCH PEOPLE TO MAKE THE PILGRIMAGE TO FONTAINEBLEAU. THEY WILL LEARN TO RESPECT, ADMIRE, AND LOVE THE FRANCE OF BYGONE DAYS THAT GAVE BIRTH TO THESE WONDERS."*
> Anatole France

The small theater built by Napoleon III.

## The Name "Fontainebleau"

♥ The town of Fontainebleau is said to have been named after a fountain called Bliaud, then Belle Eau (beautiful water). The fountain is located at the far end of the English garden.

The chapel in the château.

 The Fontainebleau forest is a vast 54,000-acre (22,000-ha) park planted with oak, beech, and pine. It is the perfect place for taking long walks near Paris.

## A World-Famous Site

The exceptional nature of the Château de Fontainebleau, its garden, and its many treasures was officially recognized in 1981, when it was added to UNESCO's list of World Heritage sites.

# • PRACTICAL INFORMATION •

## OPENING HOURS
**Château**
<u>April to September:</u> Open daily 9:30 a.m.–6 p.m.
<u>October to March:</u> Open daily 9:30 a.m.–5 p.m.
**Gardens**
<u>November to February:</u> Open daily 9 a.m.–5 p.m.
<u>March, April, and October:</u> Open daily 9 a.m.–6 p.m.
<u>May to September:</u> Open daily 9 a.m.–7 p.m.

## TICKETS
Free entry to the gardens
<u>Château:</u> €14 | reduced price €12 | free for visitors under 18 and EU citizens under 26

## GETTING THERE
Fontainebleau-Avon (train line R), then bus 1 to Château; or Melun
(RER D or train line R), then bus Express 34 to Château

## AMENITIES AND ACTIVITIES
*Jeu de paume* court
Row boats
Carriage rides
Guided tours
Tourist train

Concerts
Conferences and exhibitions
  during the Festival
  d'Histoire de l'Art, in June

chateaudefontainebleau.fr/en/

# 24

# CHÂTEAU
# de Vaux-le-Vicomte
## Maincy

*Vaux-le-Vicomte was the dream of Nicolas Fouquet (1615–1680),*
*Louis XIV's superintendent of finances, but he never had time to enjoy it.*
*A jewel designed by the three artists most representative*
*of France's Grand Siècle—architect Louis Le Vau, painter Charles Le Brun,*
*and landscape designer André Le Nôtre—this early version*
*of Versailles, as it was described by French philosopher*
*and writer Bernard Teyssèdre, can now be admired by all.*

## LE NÔTRE INVENTED HIS IMPRESSIVE ART OF PERSPECTIVE HERE.

Vaux-le-Vicomte is an *oeuvre totale*—a total work of art—created by Le Nôtre, Le Brun, and Le Vau at the request of Nicolas Fouquet, an ambitious statesman who loved beautiful things. The château, embellished with sumptuous frescoes, was designed to be closely connected to the garden, which is replete with sculptures and water features. Fouquet's vision could be summarized as follows: art everywhere, all the time. His emblem, the squirrel, is visible in certain bas-reliefs that decorate the château. Here, Le Nôtre demonstrated the full extent of his talent. The grounds at Vaux-le-Vicomte are often considered to be the archetype of the French garden. And it is indeed one of the most accomplished incarnations of the style, which spread throughout Europe in the second half of the 17th century. Of course, a French garden entails rigor and symmetry: the rectangular parterres are arranged around two paths running on perfect north-south and east-west axes. However, although geometry is omnipresent in the landscape, there is also plenty of creative whimsy. Le Nôtre used optical science to enthrall visitors: the garden is a series of illusions and surprises. The many water displays are supplied by an impressive gravity-powered pipe network measuring nearly 5 miles (8 km) in length.

Parliamentarian Nicolas Fouquet acquired Vaux-le-Vicomte in 1641, when he was just 26 years old. However, troubles with The Fronde—a revolt led by aristocrats—kept him away from the property for many years, and work only really began in 1656. The undertaking took on considerable proportions: three villages were displaced, and clearing the land of trees required the participation of thousands of workers. In 1661, it was practically finished. The result was a marvel, but a shadow was cast over this success by a dramatic turn of events. •

# The Plot

........................................

*Due to his loyalty to the royal family—*
*especially during The Fronde—*
*Nicolas Fouquet quickly became one*
*of the most important statesmen in France.*

........................................

He was appointed superintendent of finances in 1659 and, even though he had a tendency to confuse the state's coffers with his own personal fortune, he managed to straighten out the country's catastrophic economic situation. But another ambitious statesman who also moved in the highest echelons of power—Jean-Baptiste Colbert, then intendant for Cardinal Mazarin—saw Fouquet as an obstacle to his own career. He led a campaign against him in Louis XIV's court and, through his accusations, managed to sow doubt into the mind of the king.

On August 17, 1661, Fouquet held a spectacular party to unveil his château to the cream of French aristocracy, despite the fact that construction at Vaux-le-Vicomte was not quite finished. Everything was designed to dazzle the guests, including the king, who took umbrage. The event was unforgettable—so much so that it would ultimately lead to Fouquet's demise. He was unaware that a plot was being hatched against him, or if he had gotten wind of it, he chose to ignore the rumors. Three weeks later, he was

arrested for embezzlement. A momentous, three-year trial ensued during which the prosecution struggled to prove Fouquet's guilt. Despite this, he was condemned to exile, then sentenced to life imprisonment by Louis XIV. Some even believe he was the mysterious "man in the iron mask." His arrest explains why certain areas of the château were not completed, notably the ceiling in the Grand Salon, which was to be the apotheosis of Charles Le Brun's painted interior decorations. Le Brun is said to have concealed a warning to Fouquet in one of the frescoes in the games room: a squirrel (Fouquet's emblem) is being attacked by a serpent (Colbert) under the amused gaze of a lion (Louis XIV).

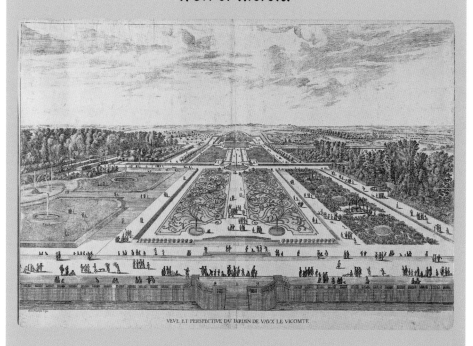

VEVE ET PERSPECTIVE DV IARDIN DE VAVX LE VICOMTE

Israël Sylvestre, *Château de Vaux-le-Vicomte,*
*View and General Perspective of the Gardens* (c. 1660).

After Fouquet's arrest, most of the statesman's possessions were seized by the king. The wife of the disgraced superintendent eventually succeeded in recovering the château, which later passed to the Duke of Villars, and then to the Duke of Praslin. The property was neglected for many years until the industrialist Alfred Sommier bought it at auction in 1875 and undertook significant restoration work. Today, it belongs to his descendants, the Vogüé family, who opened it to the public in 1968 and continue to maintain its prestige.

## Vaux-le-Vicomte's *Farnese Hercules*

Vaux-le-Vicomte's creators had planned for this sculpture to stand at the intersection of every vanishing line: from the entrance, it was even supposed to appear in the château's central archway. But it could not be installed during Nicolas Fouquet's lifetime. This reproduction was added by Alfred Sommier in the late 19th century. Hercules leans on his club after having killed the Nemean lion in an allegory of Fouquet contemplating the finished work.

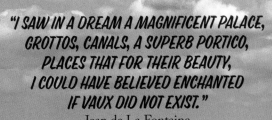

"I SAW IN A DREAM A MAGNIFICENT PALACE,
GROTTOS, CANALS, A SUPERB PORTICO,
PLACES THAT FOR THEIR BEAUTY,
I COULD HAVE BELIEVED ENCHANTED
IF VAUX DID NOT EXIST."

Jean de La Fontaine

# A PROMENADE FULL OF SURPRISES

→ Walking through Vaux-le-Vicomte, visitors are guided by a perspective measuring more than 1.2 miles (2 km) in length, interspersed with multiple discoveries. The first artworks appear at the main gate, which is guarded by fierce terms: pillars adorned with busts representing two-headed figures.

→ The walk continues through the outer forecourt, then the main courtyard, before arriving at the château. Surrounded by moats, the building reflects architectural principles that were quite unheard of at the time. Louis Le Vau played on the different volumes and enormous pilasters to create contrasts between light and shadow on the facades. A majestic dome inspired by Italian architecture tops

the central Grand Salon, around which all the other rooms are arranged. The interiors are still furnished and decorated in 17th-century style.

→ The two symmetrical parterres located in front of the château were once bedecked with intricate box tree arabesques, but they fell victim to disease and were replaced by aluminum motifs created by artist Patrick Hourcade. On the right is a flowerbed that is generally covered by plants forming a charming palette of pinks, whites, and blues, from May to October. On the left, a striking pool decorated with a gilded crown was built in tribute to Louis XIV. Who knows if he appreciated seeing this emblem in the garden of a man who was accused of taking himself for king?

> *"THE KING HAD GOOD REASON TO BE ANGRY; AT VAUX-LE-VICOMTE, HE WAS IN THE FRENCH GARDEN PAR EXCELLENCE."*
> Alain Baraton

⤖ Visitors then come to a round pool that marks the intersection of the north-south and east-west axes. Two small canals, which are invisible from the château, run alongside this perpendicular path.

⤖ After passing between two large ponds, visitors finally come upon the reflecting pool—the climax of the display. Le Nôtre calculated its position so that visitors could see either the statue of Hercules or the château reflected on its surface, depending on which side of the pool they were standing on. Another surprise: the sudden appearance of a canal measuring over a half-mile (1 km) long.

⤖ A waterfall and grottos stand on either side of the canal. This type of decoration was very fashionable in the 17th century. Conducive to contemplation, the grottos also illustrate the complex relationship between nature and culture. The sculptures of river-gods by Mathieu Lespagnandelle resemble concretions shaped by water.

⤖ The perspective ends with the Bassin de la Gerbe, where a horn of plenty produces a gracious stream of water, and with a statue of Hercules that reigns over the estate.

♥ Today, Vaux-le-Vicomte is alive and well, and welcomes visitors from around the world. The château stables are home to a carriage museum where visitors can observe horse-drawn coaches and carts from every era. In summer, the château owners host evening events, when the garden is illuminated with thousands of candles. Fans of period clothing can take part in a costume day, which is usually held in June.

## A Foreshadowing of Versailles

☞ According to a widely held belief, Louis XIV turned so violently on Fouquet because he was jealous of his incredible estate. The historical reality is more complicated, however. Nevertheless, several years later, the king, like Fouquet, called on Le Vau, Le Nôtre, and Le Brun to build the Château de Versailles. His keen aesthetic sense had no doubt recognized a true masterpiece in Vaux-le-Vicomte.

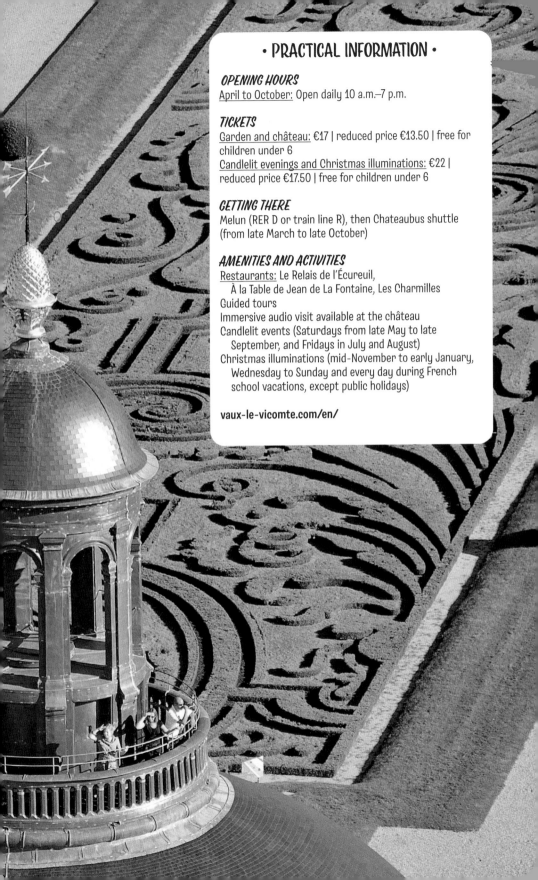

## • PRACTICAL INFORMATION •

### OPENING HOURS
<u>April to October:</u> Open daily 10 a.m.–7 p.m.

### TICKETS
<u>Garden and château:</u> €17 | reduced price €13.50 | free for children under 6
<u>Candlelit evenings and Christmas illuminations:</u> €22 | reduced price €17.50 | free for children under 6

### GETTING THERE
Melun (RER D or train line R), then Chateaubus shuttle (from late March to late October)

### AMENITIES AND ACTIVITIES
<u>Restaurants:</u> Le Relais de l'Écureuil,
   À la Table de Jean de La Fontaine, Les Charmilles
Guided tours
Immersive audio visit available at the château
Candlelit events (Saturdays from late May to late
   September, and Fridays in July and August)
Christmas illuminations (mid-November to early January,
   Wednesday to Sunday and every day during French
   school vacations, except public holidays)

vaux-le-vicomte.com/en/

# MUSÉE-JARDIN
# Bourdelle
## Égreville

*What better gallery is there to display sculptures than a garden?*
*In the 1960s, Rhodia Dufet-Bourdelle and her husband,*
*Michel Dufet, created a natural setting in Égreville to showcase*
*the works of sculptor Antoine Bourdelle (1861–1929).*
*Now open to visitors, the garden is home to about 50 statues*
*and bas-reliefs, accentuated by trees, shrubs, and flowerbeds.*

## A WORK OF ART BUILT AROUND THE WORKS OF A GREAT SCULPTOR.

The garden, which covers over 75,000 square feet (7,000 m²) was designed to resemble an artwork. The plants were carefully chosen to harmonize in form and color with the bronze sculptures: art never encroaches on nature and vice versa. Most of the works on view in the garden are casts dating from the second half of the 20th century. Although their subjects vary greatly—monumental allegories, mythological characters, portraits of major historical figures, animals—these statues all bear the mark of Antoine Bourdelle's inimitable style.

Just after passing through the front gate, visitors enter the "front" garden, where a statue of Hercules the archer dominates the scene from among a bed of red roses. The tension that the sculptor succeeded in expressing through the figure's posture is impressive: Hercules prepares to shoot an arrow to kill the birds on Lake Stymphalia—horrible monsters with an appetite for human flesh. The intricate box tree arabesques, which stand out against brightly colored backgrounds, form refined patterns of labyrinths and palmettes. Visitors reach the "back" garden by walking around the farmhouse, the estate's main building. Lawns with sophisticated contours are interspersed with shrubs pruned in parallelepiped or other forms and are lined with flowers that bring the landscape to life with their myriad colors. The varieties are regularly renewed: depending on the time of the year, the garden is home to roses, peonies, violets, daffodils, anemones, crocuses, hellebores, and primroses. In spring, this enchanting scene is enhanced by the blossoms of a cherry tree and a Japanese quince tree, then of a purple magnolia. The centerpiece of this area is the decorative vegetable garden, whose walkways and paths form a regular grid. In the center, a statue, *Serpent*, evokes the Devil, who persuaded Eve to taste the

forbidden fruit in the garden of Eden. In front of the garden, a woman holding fruit (Eve?) stands before a statue of a despairing Adam, who turns his back to her. He has probably just learned that he is about to be driven out of Paradise. At the end of the garden stands a monument to General Alvear, an Argentinean statesman who worked for South American independence in the 19th century. Behind him, a splendid weeping cedar frames the perspective. •

## ANTOINE BOURDELLE

Early in his career, Antoine Bourdelle was strongly influenced by the work of Auguste Rodin, for whom he worked as an assistant for several years. This was so apparent in his early sculptures that at first critics nicknamed him the "half-Rodin." Over time, he managed to free himself from this influence and develop a unique style. He readily distanced himself from realism to give greater strength to the expressions of his figures. Fascinated by Greco-Roman sculpture, he gradually sought to synthesize forms and lines to confer a greater expressive power on his works: "Contain, maintain, master are the rules of construction."

*Serpent* (1925) and *Large Dying Centaur* (1914).

*Adam* (1889).

*Hercules the Archer* (1909).

*The Fruit* (1902–1906).

*Beethoven, Large Leaning Bust* (1909).
Bourdelle identified with Beethoven, who was a visionary genius, but also a tormented man.

## MUSÉE BOURDELLE IN PARIS

➥ Visitors can learn more about the work of this great sculptor in his former studio in Montparnasse, which was transformed into a museum after his death. It, too, is surrounded by beautiful gardens decorated with bronze statues.

# An Art Deco Garden

☞ The large axes around which the garden is organized and the symmetry of the parterres might call to mind the French-style gardens at Versailles or at Vaux-le-Vicomte, but the ubiquitous geometric motifs are more reminiscent of the art deco style. This setting is particularly suited to the works of Antoine Bourdelle—their monumental size and their references to antiquity connect them to the art deco movement.

## A BIT OF HISTORY

☞ Before being acquired by Rhodia Bourdelle-Dufet and Michel Dufet, the plot on which the garden-museum is located was primarily farmland. The couple made it into their second home, as well as a space dedicated to preserving the memory of Antoine Bourdelle. Michel Dufet, an architect and interior designer, created the garden between 1966 and 1972 as a way to showcase the sculptures that were gradually added to it. His artistic sensibility is palpable in the association of geometric forms and the touches of color that structure the garden. It resembles a painting when seen from above. Dufet also succeeded in giving each sculpture enough space to blend harmoniously into the surrounding environment. After his death in 1985, the garden gradually deteriorated. When Rhodia died in 2002, she left the estate to the Seine-et-Marne département and it was turned into an outdoor museum accessible to the public. The spirit with which the former owners had infused the garden was revived through an ambitious restoration project led by landscape architect Françoise Phiquepal.

## • PRACTICAL INFORMATION •

### OPENING HOURS
April 1 to October 31: Open Wednesday to Sunday
10:30 a.m.–1 p.m. and 2 p.m.–6 p.m.

### TICKETS
Garden and museum: €5 | reduced price €3 | free for
visitors under 18

### GETTING THERE
Melun (RER D or train line R), then bus Express 34 to
Piscine; or Nemours Saint-Pierre (TER 5911), then bus
10 to Edmond Hubert

### AMENITIES AND ACTIVITIES
Guided tours (booking required)
Introductory sculpture and drawing workshops for
    adults and children; booklets and games for children

**musee-jardin-bourdelle.fr/fr** (in French)

## FRENCH EDITION

**Design & illustrations**
Amélie du Petit Thouars

**Editorial director**
Julie Rouart,
assisted by Adèle Ehlinger

**Administration manager**
Delphine Montagne

**Editorial contributions**
Catherine Laulhère-Vigneau
and Yaël Rusé

**Picture research**
Marie Audet

## ENGLISH EDITION

**Editorial Director**
Kate Mascaro

**Editor**
Helen Adedotun

**Translation from the French**
Kate Robinson

**Copyediting**
Victorine Lamothe

**Typesetting**
Claude-Olivier Four

**Proofreading**
Nicole Foster

**Production**
Julie Hautecourt

**Color separation**
Les Caméléons, Paris

Printed in Slovakia by TBB

Originally published in French
as *Mon Paris des plus beaux jardins*
© Éditions Flammarion, Paris, 2023
© "Silence, ça pousse" France
Télévisions, 2023

English-language edition
© Éditions Flammarion, Paris, 2024
© "Silence, ça pousse" France
Télévisions, 2024

Éditions Flammarion
82 Rue Saint-Lazare
75009 Paris

editions.flammarion.com
@flammarioninternational

24 25 26   3 2 1

ISBN: 978-2-08-044723-4

Legal Deposit: 06/2024

# Credits (t: top; b: bottom; l: left; r: right; c: center)